Trumpets of
God

By

N. M YLVISAKER

Published by Augsburg Publishing House Minneapolis

239
YL6I

BOOKS BY THE AUTHOR

THE GLORY ROAD	1933
FACES TOWARD GOD	1936
NO OTHER WAY	1938
SERVICE PRAYER BOOK	1940
TRUMPETS OF GOD	1945

22999
May 47

Printed and manufactured in the United States of America by the
Augsburg Publishing House, Minneapolis 15, Minnesota

TO MY PARENTS

*Who, listening here, heard
the trumpets of God and
went home to glory*

*"If the trumpet give an uncertain sound,
who shall prepare himself to the battle?"*

(I Corinthians 14:8)

"The dialectical structure which he erected, he could
not dedicate to any human being, much less to himself.
If he should dedicate it to anyone, it would have to be
to Providence, to whom, indeed, it was consecrated, day
after day, year after year, by the author, who, to speak
historically, died of a mortal disease, but, to speak poet-
ically, died of a longing for Eternity, where he desires
nothing better than that he might there uninterruptedly
give thanks unto God."

(Kierkegaard)

*"This is the end of philosophy:
to know that we must believe."*

(Geibel)

Foreword

TRUMPETS OF GOD is not intended to be just another book. It is not another theological book, although there is theology in it, as we dare hope. It is not even only another religious book, of which the world has so many which are never read. It is a book which faces life with you and which tries to help you find God.

There has been, in spite of every consideration to the contrary, a great urge to write this book, even though it may reach only very few of those for whom it is primarily intended. We hope and pray that it may prove helpful to those who do discover its intentions.

Søren Kierkegaard, the Danish thinker and religious philosopher, delighted in addressing so many of his books, particularly those which were to convey a religious message, to "the individual." It was his way of indicating that there were individuals who needed his message and the help it contained.

If anything, TRUMPETS OF GOD has a message to "the individual"—to the individual or individuals who in this generation of disappointed hopes, tragic despair, and lost gods find themselves floundering about in the world without God and without hope.

This book tries to sound the trumpet call of God to these lost individuals not to yield to cynicism and despair. There is a way out. It goes by way of discovering again discarded truths about Him who saves to the uttermost, who Himself goes by the name of "Way, and Truth, and Life." This book will try to show you the unreasonableness of unbelief, the tragedy of doubt, the certainty of the assurance of faith, the strong foundation of conviction, and the sure hope which is theirs who follow Him who is still life eternal.

Yesterday too many of our leaders and teachers helped you to lose God. Today, amidst the awful horrors of war, you are discovering the universal need for God. But "foxhole religion" is not enough. That tends only to prove to you that there is a God. Your release from fear, the fear of death and the fear of facing God, who has been offended by a world full of sin, is gained only by way of Him whom God has revealed as the Savior.

You must know Him, you must see Him, you must make—for yourself—the discovery of who He is and what He has done for you. No other knowledge or discovery means anything—in the face of death and eternity.

It is the hope of this book to show you, in its humble way, even in a world which still ridicules and denies, how necessary is this discovery, and how satisfying and eternally saving is the knowledge gained, if you want to possess "the peace of God which passeth all understanding."

It is time for the sounding of trumpets to be heard in a lost world. It is time "the trumpets of God" be sounded so clearly that all may hear. It is time that men stop and listen to the call; and, listening, face the great Either/Or of life: either a life continuing without God, which will bring on the greater tragedy of world judgment; or a life finding God, which leads to everlasting peace.

Minneapolis, Minn.   N. M. Y.
Pentecost Day, 1944

Contents

Contents

A Time to Sound
the Trumpets of God

It happened in the long ago, but it might as well have been yesterday. Indeed, our yesterdays are like the long, long time ago of years that are gone.

It all seemed so impossible, so utterly futile as to belong in the category of the absurd; but faith is like that: its foundations are laid in the realms men call the absurd.

It was in a day of marching men, of the noise and clamor of war; and the trumpets were used to sound the advance or the retreat.

But these were the "trumpets of God" which were sounded, and the trumpets of God never sound retreat. They are blown to signal advance. They are sounded to proclaim triumph, victory. They sound in honor of Him who made us and all things. And before His throne of glory their song of triumph shall be heard from generation to generation—forevermore.

"Trumpets of God" are sounded, too, in judgment and

condemnation when nations and peoples know not the day of their visitation.

They were priests of God who carried the trumpets before the walls of Jericho that day. Around and around the walls of this ancient stronghold of paganism they circled, with their people following, the chosen people of God. Once each day the trumpets sounded and then there came each day the silence of impending doom.

Till that seventh day, which still is included in the joke columns of men who have never known and never wanted to know the wisdom of God, and the power of God, and the glory of God. Then suddenly it all happened. The trumpets sounded, not once, but at each of the seven turns the people of Israel made around the doomed city. The trumpets sounded as only the trumpets of God can sound, and back of them was the overwhelming power of God. And the people shouted, a shout like the accumulated voice of disaster, and back of it was the wrath and judgment of God. And God performed His miracle. The walls, impregnable like yesterday's Maginot and Siegfried and Mannerheim and Stalin lines, crumbled before the judgment of God, and His righteous wrath moved against the people of Jericho and among them till the city was no more.

Jericho, the city of sin! Jericho, the city of doom! Jericho, the city of judgment and wrath! Struck down that day by the miracle of the "trumpets of God"!

They still call it impossible. They laugh and mock, all those who believe not God. Before the might of God they ridicule, those who recognize only the futility of men.

Impossible? But the impossibility of man becomes the possibility of God. The futility of unbelief becomes, for those who are God's the possibility of faith. For faith still rests on the dynamic of God, on the miracle of God, on the convincing truth of God. And God's truth it is

that He forever lives and moves with insistent majesty
and power though all the world crumble into dust before Him.

It was in the long ago of yesterday God moved thus
with His power. But His trumpets still are sounding,
sounding ever clearer above the din of war and misery
and judgment and sin. And out from these judgments
there comes still the voice of prophets telling people
about their sin, about God, and about victories which
can be won, if sin is disowned and confessed and repented. Out from the presence of God there come
Joshuas still who in the face of every need cry out with
the voice of God who sent them:

"Up, sanctify the people, and say, Sanctify yourselves
against tomorrow. For thus saith the Lord God of Israel,
There is an accursed thing in the midst of thee, O Israel:
thou canst not stand before thine enemies, until ye take
away the accursed thing from among you" (Joshua 7:13).

I think that is the world's great need today, and America's need: to sanctify ourselves against tomorrow, to take
away every accursed thing that separates us from God
and causes the judgments of God. And the trumpets of
God are sounding loudly above all the chaos and disaster and agony and tears of war: and the sound I hear
tells me that all of us need to turn back again to God,
who alone can release us from the madness of our sins.
As Roger Babson has said,

The need of the hour is not more money, more real estate,
more stocks and bonds, but more self-control, more unselfishness, more faith, and more courage. Self-control, unselfishness,
faith, and courage are spiritual qualities, and these come only
with vital religion.

People today need above all the ability of right choices,
and right choices come with a wisdom which only religion can give.

So America's great need today is in the realm of the spiritual. Too long she has been feeding at the fleshpots of comfort and ease and pleasure and the shoddy things of life. All about her there is ruin and chaos and suffering and catastrophe and despair, and still she listens, almost unbelievably, to the siren voices of indifference and apathy and listlessness when in her ears are sounding the trumpets of God calling her and all who would live to the courage and faith of great men of God. Loudly the trumpets call: "Have faith!"

> Have faith—
> That Time shall strike the shackles from us all
> When we have learned to conquer from within,
> And hail the bombs of circumstance that fall
> To blast our self-sufficient house of sin.
>
> Who fears the haughty tyrant's blustering wrath—
> Whose breath is as the passing winds that blow?
> God is not mocked—His hand still carves the path
> Victims and conquerors alike must go!
>
> In vain we build our ramparts in the skies
> Against a peril from across the seas
> If in ourselves the greater danger lies
> Of self-assurance couched on beds of ease.
>
> What bomb-proof shelters shall we seek from greed,
> What cannon forge against our own deceit?
> In what defensive armor rests our need
> When Equity lies bound beneath our feet?
>
> God raise up Jeremiahs for our day
> To breathe His righteous Spirit o'er our land.
> God give us wisdom to desire His Way—
> To build our house on something more than sand!
>
> (E. Theodore Nelson)

Something more than sand!

That is the trumpet call. That is the voice of America today and especially the voice of the youth of America to us whom God expects to guide and lead, to help them to build their house on more than sand. Or haven't you heard their voice, the insistent voice of their great need as it comes out from the catastrophe of the epochal decision they must make? What an awful tragedy if they have cried out for help and we to whom they cry have no ears to hear!

"Take us back to solid ground," they cry. Or such was the title, at any rate, of a startling editorial which recently appeared in the *Daily Iowan,* the student paper of the University of Iowa. "Take us back to solid ground," it said. "That is the hope, and the plea of American students everywhere."

And then this young student laid bare his soul, a soul disturbed and distressed and lost and despairing.

We are looking forward to the America we'll have when this war is over. Who doubts that the burdens of our generation then will be the greatest in our history? What facts will we have to recognize then that you and we—of both generations —may just as well be facing now?

We are speaking to the faculty and the administration of universities and colleges across the land—because the American people have the right to look to you for leadership.

The rank and file of us have never been trained in how to live.

You haven't taught us to be able to take it.

We are not living within our means; we followed your example.

We're afraid of hard work; you never taught us to love it.

We can't accept responsibility; you couldn't before us.

We don't know the meaning of discipline; you didn't discipline us.

What are you going to do about it? You can't just let it go, and leave our generation ignorant of the means of living, to make your mistakes all over again, to muddle through other crises.

We have grown tired to death of smatterings of knowledge, dispensed by professors and instructors hired to teach that smattering and nothing more. We want to get our teeth into something vibrant and alive, something permanent, something which ties the present to the truths of the glorious past. We want discipline in the job of living.

You've got to go back to solid ground again. You've got to start thinking again in terms of men and women, not in terms of degrees; in terms of knowledge, complete and directed, and not in terms of the number of courses on the curriculum.

Forget that training in the spiritual elements of life is to be found, technically, in the academic course numbers of the school of religion, or in the profound teachings of philosophy, or in the church. We want constant things of life, the physical, mental, and spiritual things which have been the foundations of humanity since the civilization of ancient China. We want it in every course, in every department, in every college. We want it every day! We want it as the backbone of higher education, the thing to which all else is tied and of which all else is a part. It's in medicine and commerce and physics, too, and those of you who teach medicine and commerce and physics must teach religion as well. It isn't outside your field! That willingness to believe that it is has cost us untold unhappiness and misery. You are dealing with knowledge, not just an isolated bit of it, but all of it, whatever your field. You are training men and women—not machines—beings who think and move and react to stimuli and upon whom you have tremendous influence because of that.

If that were the cry only of an individual student facing the realities of life, we might pass him by with an indifferent shrug of the shoulder as did the priest and the Levite the man fallen among thieves.

But this isn't the cry of an individual. It is the cry of America, of thousands and tens of thousands of students and of youth who have fed on the husks of the evolutionistic and materialistic philosophy of life, and now in the presence of a crumbling civilization know no place to which to turn for help to find the way of life which satisfies and saves.

It was Dorothy Thompson, columnist, who helped to show us the tragedy confronting us. And how effectively she did it!

She published a letter sent by an undergraduate of one of our greatest Eastern universities to the president of that institution. Miss Thompson has the good sense to let this letter stand without comment as she gives it the space allotted her usual column, for, she says, "Better than anything else I have read, it sums up the dilemma of our 'educated' youth today."

You, sir, were brought up from earliest childhood in an atmosphere of traditional Christianity and democracy. You read, learned, and inwardly digested the Bible. Nearly every Sunday you went to church, and there you heard and believed sermons which postulated the divinity of Christ, eternal principles of right and wrong, the existence of the human soul, a personal God and a life after death. Thanks to your early training, your life as you have led it derives its meaning largely from the teachings of Jesus.

During your youth you also were educated to think that man is superior to animals, that he is a free agent capable of choosing between good and evil. Loyalty to country was an ideal you came to cherish, and your schooling never caused you to doubt that man possesses certain inalienable rights. Your position is typical of your generation.

But what about us, the youth of America? What have we been taught to revere in the university you direct, and in other similar institutions throughout the land?

Then he goes on to show how in the modern college Christianity has progressively lost its grip on young minds; how youth today hardly ever looks at the Bible; how sociology has taught that morals are relative to time and place, that there can really be no such thing as sin.

From their professors they have been taught, he says, that religions are the product of myth and superstition and that there are no gods except such as man creates for himself; that no scientist has ever isolated the soul in his laboratory and so there can be no soul.

In political systems you teach us, he continues, that man is distinct from animals, and still our biology courses now conceive of man merely as one species of animal. How shall we differentiate between the doctrine of free will and the doctrine of determinism?

Personally, I fail to understand how you, or any other college president, can expect us to become ardent Christians and democrats when the vital postulates on which these faiths are supposed to rest are daily undermined in the classrooms.

Then out from the despair of this great American tragedy through which he has lost the way to the great realities of life, he cries out:

Isn't it palpably obvious to you that at the root of the trouble lies an apparent contradiction between the implications of our studies and the ideals we are expected to revere? Of course we are apathetic, discontented, reluctant to assume the responsibility of thinking and acting. Of course we live solely in the present, without visions of the future, without any firm convictions, hiding under a mask of conventional behavior the "futilitarianism" the more thoughtful of us clearly recognize, the less thoughtful profoundly sense. Of course our feet are a thousand miles off the ground. We, the young, are the American tragedy.

Some of our elders have wondered why we are not more excited over totalitarian aggression and ruthlessness. But for most of us the international situation is ultimately a case of one group of animals without rights or free will torturing another group of the same breed. No Promethean fires of faith and sacrificial zeal burn in our hearts. Our wishy-washy adherence to Christianity and democracy pales into nothingness

along-side the incredible devotion of German youths to the
Nazi creed. You may as well face the brute fact that our education has made the difference between us and you far more
deep-striking and revolutionary than any normal variation in
generations.

Our situation has indeed grown more serious than you think.
Your generation must soon pass on to our hands the torch of
democracy and Christianity. Our hearts impel us to be faithful to that trust, but our heads that you have helped condition
may decree otherwise. As men think, as men view the cosmos
and human nature, so they must act. And when the time
comes for us to act, we may embitter your declining years. We
may destroy the liberal values toward which man has struggled
down through the ages.

If we are to be saved, our elders must assist us to harmonize
our education with the old faith. Perhaps you will say that
every individual should grapple courageously with the facts by
himself, that no one can do our thinking for us. Quite so.
Yet surely with all the richness of your experience, with all
your achievements, you and others like you can at least comment helpfully on the demoralizing naturalism and relativism
that render us impotent to face the present world crisis. It
would seem that America has grave need for a brand-new
humanitarian philosophy based upon modern developments
in the arts and sciences. Callow youth cannot conjure up such
a philosophy without guidance.

If our outlook is ever to rise above a selfish materialism,
somehow, somewhere, *we must find an answer to our questions.**

Find an answer to our questions!

But the intellectual chaos of which both of these individual students through their searching and despairing
appeals give only too much evidence is only a part of
that appalling catastrophe which is affecting with such
tragic realism our whole fabric of civilization. It is after
all only a part of that greater collapse which has all but
destroyed our ethical principles, our morality, our religious life, and all our spirituality. Our personal relations,

*Quoted with permission, *Ladies Home Journal.*

our community life, our national and international relationships have all been affected—to such an extent indeed
that internationally it is no longer possible seemingly to
make treaties predicated on such previously generally
accepted virtues as honesty, honor, reliability—promises
to be governed in the future by commitments solemnly
covenanted. Would anyone after the tragic experience of
Poland, Norway, Holland, Russia ever be tempted to
trust the given word of a Hitler or a Mussolini or any
of their henchmen? Would anyone after the awful tragedy
of Pearl Harbor ever be led to believe the pledged word
of representatives of atheistic Japan?

Nations and peoples become immoral in their relationships when religion has been disowned. For morality and
religion are concomitant parts of a fabric which together,
not separately, govern a man's philosophy of life. Without religion, morality just doesn't exist.

Perhaps it has taken the tragedy of a present world
conflict to make this clear. No longer do men speak with
the bold confidence of a decade ago about their ability to
face the issues of life without God. Or if they do, there
is in their assertion only the cold cynicism of despair because they feel that the world which they have known has
failed them in an hour of awful need.

There came to me the other day a letter from one of
our university trained service men which better than anything I have seen in print reveals the hopelessness of such
despair.

This well educated, intellectually honest representative
of our defense armies wrote in language I shall not forget:

It is appalling the number who profess that the "Faith of our
Fathers" is obsolescent and . . . hypocritical! And these are
not illiterate draftees either, these men who laugh politely at
such things as Holy Communion and Confirmation. Passé . . .
they regard it! The Theses on the doors of the Wittenberg

Church . . . passé! I know what they feel and think and study
. . . I live among these fine, healthy men. They are mostly
men with broken, fashionably-modern home backgrounds. They
are some of the finest blood of our nation! Don't you feel as
I do, *something* must be done to *help* these boys?

Pastor, as you may know . . . *This* is the *eleventh* hour . . .
This is the staircase of time that leads right up to the brink
of Mars. The next turn in this staircase is stinking, ugly hell.

Now is the time for you pastors to work . . . [soldier language
here cannot be repeated] . . . to save, to build, to satisfy these
trainees for this terrible tomorrow.

Yes, we wrote to him, . . . right away! And he wrote
back:

A mighty fortress is our God! And we need you leaders of
men to gently maneuver us toward this fortress. The day your
letter arrived I was ready to give up in desperation. "Was my
self-imposed mission an impracticable ideal?" I asked myself.
But your answer was a light from Him. Thank you for such
generous encouragement and understanding; for the supplies
of literature, the Chaplain and I are most happy and grateful.
May your able direction and firm handclasp give us new
strength to dint this darkness of the time, and to "keep close
to God."

Or would you perhaps want to look at another letter,
which came from one of our pastors this time, telling a
story which may haunt you, as it will me, till the end of
life? Yes, it's authentic. The pastor who writes vouches
for that! But don't read on, if you think the church or
you have no responsibilities in this present emergency. It
may shock you too much for your own complacency.

I shall never forget this youth. Let us call him Joe. He was
one of the outstanding young men of the congregation, devot-
ed to the church, member of the choir; a tall, handsome, and
winsome youth whom everybody liked. I took to him from the
first, and he seemed to take to me. We had many conversations.

His age was about 21. His father was a deacon of the church.

Then one day I learned that he had suddenly left home, to join the army as a volunteer in order not to be drafted. We all missed him very much. To keep in contact with him and to cheer him, I wrote to him a few times as the months passed by. Then one weekend he came home on furlough, and that Sunday morning I saw him in the church at the service, sitting there in the pew with his folks, as true to a picture of a soldier as one would wish to look at in his new uniform, erect, stern-visaged. At the door after the service I met him and shook his hand, and have never received such a shock as I did then. For as I greeted him and asked how he was, he ignored my hand, raised his hand in the military salute, with never a fleeting smile on his stern, sad face. Then he passed on. To him in that moment I apparently was but as a stranger. And we had been such good friends when last we had met—before he had left for camp. I found that everybody else was as surprised by the change in him as I was. The next day, being Monday, he left for camp.

A couple of weeks later I met his sister and asked about Joe. She told me that in his every letter home he complained about being very lonely and homesick. And then, just a few days later, his father received a telegram that Joe had committed suicide in camp, "the cause unknown."

The news of it stirred the whole community, and no funeral there has been more widely attended nor sadder than when this promising youth of such tragic end was laid to his final rest.

Suicide! "Cause unknown." There was no morbid trait in Joe's nature. On the contrary he was of an eminently cheerful disposition and of a well-balanced mind; of the best of habits, companionships and home-surroundings. A youth of that type does not readily take his own life. Yet, perhaps the cause and motive of his desperate act can be traced to the very contrasts of his home-life and that he had to face in the camp.

Pastors, parents, go to your utmost to stand by our young men in the camps. For if ever in life, they need it just there.

All the while the answer has been and is here for all,

even the most disillusioned and lost. And the answer is all wrapped up in the great dynamic of the Christian religion and in Him who to bring it gave Himself to the uttermost that we in Him might learn to live.

It is this dynamic, the power of Jesus Christ, so freely given, the world and we need, and need desperately right now. It is the only power which can bring us out of our own selfishness, our hatreds, our wars, and our chaotic ways.

Strange to say, it is this power which in these catastrophic days we imagined had all been lost, which men are beginning to discover again as the new prophets of God who have themselves felt its consuming power go about revealing it to others.

I have seen them as with incredible fortitude they face the issues and themselves live as evidences of its regenerating influence. Great men of God they are, teachers, pastors, chaplains, Christian workers, who, disdaining all ridicule and the defeatism of the past, go out on their ministry where the old Gospel is their only way of life. That Gospel is their only message. That is their only power. That their only glory. And He who saves to the uttermost walks with them and works miracles as they go.

Oh, the miracles this Christ still can perform! And, oh, the glory of that Book which today in millions of copies is finding its way into great army camps and into lands where persecution today is sure for those who dare to read its sacred pages!

For men are finding God again and God's Christ again. They are finding reality in the life He gives. And in Him there is salvation and in Him there is power: power to believe, power to live, power to serve, power to die. There is a miracle in His name which can make the young soldier say: "Chaplain, they can take away all I have. But I'll never let them take my prayer book. Not ever."

I questioned one who stood at the world's far crossroads:
"Which is the way that leads to Eternal Light?"
And he lifted his eyes to the hills ahead and answered:
"Yonder it lies, and the Guide is still in sight."
"Who is this Guide?" I asked, and he answered: "Jesus."
"Who is this Jesus of whom I have never heard?"
And there to a lost, distressed and bewildered comrade,
He told of the Savior, word by precious word.

I left behind me the dark and troubled valley.
I took the Glory Way, and found Him there:
A lamp to my feet, a radiance to my pathway,
And ever within my heart I am aware
That I might have missed the way at the far-off crossroads,
If one had failed me who had the words to say,
And I shall cry aloud to each hesitant pilgrim:
"Follow your Leader!" "Follow the Glory Way."

(The Glory Way by Grace Noll Crowell)

Trumpets of God! Trumpets of God!

But the trumpets must give a *certain* sound, so we through faith may gird ourselves to the battle. The battle is to the death. But through death, the road leads to life!

And beyond? Even now you hear the echo the pilgrim of *Pilgrim's Progress* heard one day of "trumpets sounding from the other side"!

This Unbelieving World

MORE than half of the people of our country are not reached by the message of the church. They are not Christian. Indeed, they have no religion at all. They have no faith in God. They even boast of their unbelief, and glory in it.

And in the world everywhere men and women have forsaken and forgotten God.

There is no greater delusion in life than the delusion of unbelief. For with unbelief you strangle every incentive for creative action, as you strangle life itself. There is neither a future nor any hope for the future in unbelief. Unbelief robs you of all there is in life, as it robs you of a place in eternal life.

I met an unbeliever the other day. A young man he was, clever, intelligent, well-read and well-informed, a graduate from the professional course of an old university. He was out to see the world. On borrowed money he left home to travel, to broaden his outlook, to add to his measure of culture. He confessed that as yet he had never done a day's work. He had no idea what self-support meant. He had been satisfied to live on the fruit of others' toil.

He had no purpose, no aim, no goal for his life. He had no idea what he wanted to do, or what he should be. Indeed, he did not care much about the morrow. He only wanted to live—now!

Then, suddenly, as he spoke to me, he remembered I was a minister. And seemingly to justify his attitude, though he was a guest in my home, he broke into a wild tirade against religion, and against God. No intelligent person could any longer believe such childishness, he said. Passé, he called it! As for him, he wanted no God, he believed in no heaven, no hell, no hereafter. All he wanted was life now, life with all the satisfaction it could offer.

No educated man believed any longer, he said. In the universities they had exploded the very idea of faith. But he forgot that others had attended universities and graduate schools, and that they might be informed even though they did not share the skepticism of unbelief.

How shocked he was when I told him to return later, after he had faced life, the cruel harshness of life, and the tragedies of life, and death. We might have something to discuss then. But not now—not now, when like the fool of the Bible he had gotten no farther than to deny the very existence of God who gives life.

He could hardly dream then, nor did I, that within six months tragedy would overwhelm him. Nor that he would be pleading with me, a minister, to save him from a life which had broken to pieces before the echoes of his boasting had died away. Nor could he possibly realize then that within a few additional months his country would be ruthlessly invaded and he himself come face to face with tragedy in the form of conqueror demands which would deprive him of all meaning to life itself.

Deny God! Deny what God has done! Just brush it all away as one would an obstinate fly! Just close your eyes and say, I don't and I won't believe!

But it isn't as simple as that!

What would you say if, in the presence of the wonders man has been able to accomplish, I should do as did the Irishman who saw the giraffe for the first time. He looked and looked and looked. Only finally to turn away in astonished disbelief: "Why, there ain't no such animal!"

Here is the San Francisco Bridge, eight miles of miraculous engineering, one of the great wonders of this present world. There the Boulder Dam before whose towering concrete walls and colossal turbine, high-powered motors, the greatest engineers stand in amazed wonder. Here are the towering skyscrapers whose steel and stone reach a thousand feet above streets where men like insignificant ants scramble about for a living. There the great cathedrals, with their lofty towers and spires, their great gothic arches—for centuries the objects of man's ceaseless struggle for architectural beauty and of his restless desire to erect temples, worthy shrines for the worship of a perfect God.

I stand transfixed by awe that such things can be. I wonder that mere man can accomplish such miracles. What a fool I would be, seeing it all, were I to stand there and deny the reality of what my eyes have beheld.

But the moment I turn to other realms where God does dwell, and where He has performed and is still performing ageless miracles—to the heavens, where is declared the wonder of His glory in sky and sun and moon and a myriad of shining stars, whose number no man has yet been able to count; to the firmament which reveals His handiwork; to the circling planets constantly moving in rhythmic regularity; and to the power that directs it all

and makes such glories possible; I say, when I turn to
these realms, must I close my eyes in unbelief, and say, I
do not believe there is a God who has made all this?

Or the other miracles of nature, showing in a thousand
ways God's majestic glory: golden sunrise and awesome
sunset; a rainbow splashing the colors of a paradise to
come across the skies; the birds which come and go with
the regularity of the seasons; the gorgeous flowers which
lift their many-colored faces from the black earth which
produced them, all smiling with the beauty of heaven;
the intricate miracle which is man; I say again, seeing all
this glory, should I still stubbornly say, I do not and I
will not believe there is a God?

One day I found a poem by Bliss Carman:

> I took a day to search for God,
> And found Him not. But as I trod
> By rocky ledge, through woods untamed,
> Just where one scarlet lily flamed,
> I saw His footprint in the sod.
>
> Then suddenly, all unaware,
> Far off in the deep shadows, where
> A solitary thrush
> Sang through the holy twilight hush—
> I heard His voice upon the air.
>
> And even as I marveled how
> God gives us Heaven here and now,
> In stir of wind that hardly shook
> The poplar leaves beside the brook—
> His hand was light upon my brow.
>
> At last with evening as I turned
> Homeward, and thought what I had learned
> And all that there was still to probe—
> I caught the glory of His robe
> Where the last fires of sunset burned.

Back to the world with quickening start
I looked and longed for any part
In making saving Beauty be . . .
And from that kindling ecstasy
I knew God dwelt within my heart.

(With the permission of Dodd, Mead & Co.,
Publishers of Mr. Carman's poems)

I fly across the mountains whose lofty peaks cry out to
each other: How wonderful is our God! I sail the oceans,
where deep calls unto deep reminding us of the majesty
and power of God. I steam through the fjords and over
the lakes. I pass a thousand waterfalls which proclaim the
glory of God and sing His praise. But seeing it all, shall I
close my eyes still and say, No, there is no God, no God at
all who created this by the power of His word!

I visit museums and libraries and ruins of former
glories. I see the Glass Flower Museum of Harvard University, the archeological museums of London, Paris,
Berlin, Rome, Herculaneum, Pompey, and Naples. Men
have tried desperately to reproduce the glories of God's
creation in glass and stone and wood. But how the copy
suffers by comparison with God's created originals in
flower or beast or man! Men accept the copy. They reject
the Maker of the original in scoffing unbelief. How
strange is man, and beyond all explanation the unreasonableness of his skepticism and denial and rejection!

Until I caught the rhythm of His life,
I hadn't heard the music of the spheres,
The simple cadence of ancient psalms,
The lyric beauty of a thousand years.

I had not seen the loveliness of dawn
Across the lifted hills, the gold and gray
Of winter sunsets, or the moonlight hush
Upon a sleeping world, or flash of spray

Against eternal rocks! And now, behold!
The voiceless future is a singing fame!
White Presences attend me everywhere,
Their canticles an echo of His name!

(Author Unknown)

And then I pick up my Bible and page it through. Its
every page startles me and commands my attention. It
speaks to me as no other book has ever done.

It ushers me at once into the great realities of life. It
brings me into the presence of God. Here is life, my life;
here is God, and this Book bids me to recognize His
presence and to choose—choose myself or God!

Like no other book, the Bible solves for me the puz-
zling realities and each demanding issue of life. It faces
the problems of life and sees them through. It tells me in
no uncertain language the answer to questions philosophers have been asking since man appeared. No answer
has ever been more complete or satisfying than the answer the Bible has given.

This Book knows me through and through. It knows
me better than I know myself. And reading it, I can
never escape from its verdict about myself. It even makes
me face myself. It forces me to do so honestly, if there is
a speck of honesty in me. And it will not let me escape
until I have solved the problem which is myself as in the
presence of God. It wants me to see and realize and
appreciate what God thinks about the person who is
myself. It makes me face God as I stand convicted by the
being who is myself.

Then I begin to see myself as God sees me. Like the
student who to begin with rebelled against religious
chapel attendance, only to accept it at last and through it
begin the study of the Bible for the first time. From his
heart he confessed at last: "Why, this Book knows me
better than I know myself; it knows my thoughts and
desires and weaknesses and sins."

That is what the Bible does. It tells us about man's rebellion against God, about sin, and about the inevitable separation from God which sin has brought about. It tells about God's righteous wrath against him who sins.

But then it tells about a miracle which never could have been discovered in the brain of man, the great miracle that goes by the strange name of "the forgiveness of sins." It tells about God's love, about Christ's redemptive work, about the possibility of salvation from sin.

And then of a sudden when the very power of God grips my soul and convinces me of the truth of what I read, and I see God and the truth of God and the beauty of the life He has called me to live in His Son, Jesus Christ—what manner of response should this be, if in the very hour of conviction and faith, I rise up, close the Book, throw it aside, reject its saving content, and say with the tragic consequence of rejection: I do not and I will not believe God could do that: make me His child and an heir of life.

I face the mysteries of life, and death. I discover that Jesus Christ explains it all, that He can and will solve all the riddles of life. He even takes me into the very chambers of death, where my loved ones are struggling with the last enemy. I see the Lord of life take them by the hand. I hear Him say to them: "I am the resurrection and the life: he that believeth in me, though he were dead, yet shall he live: And whosoever liveth and believeth in me shall never die" (John 11:25-26). And He leads them safely through the valley of the shadow of death straight into life eternal.

I have seen it all with these eyes of mine. And again and again have I seen the gospel He gave me to preach change unbelief into faith, doubt into certainty, death into life. This gospel changes lives. Transforms them. Makes heroes here. Victors over there. With joy they go through death to meet Him who is life in life everlasting.

And then you say that, seeing all this, I should go out into a hopeless and despairing world and say: No, it can't be true, I can't and I won't believe!

The patriarch Job was tempted to do that once. He doubted in his complete tragedy God, and he questioned the wisdom and the purposes of God. Do you remember God then? What God did? If you are a doubter and an unbeliever, and if you are tempted to be impressed by the cleverness and the superiority of your ability at reasoning out life and God and eternity, may I suggest that you read again and again the 38th chapter of Job and the chapters that follow, where God in language which no man could ever frame or conceive or answer reveals Himself as God and in His power and wisdom so crushes the doubting, unbelieving Job that he finally cries out in his despair and contrition: "I know that thou canst do everything and that no thought can be withholden from thee. Who is he that hideth counsel without knowledge? Therefore, have I uttered that I understood not; things too wonderful for me, which I knew not. Hear, I beseech thee, and I will speak: I will demand of thee, and declare thou unto me. I have heard of thee by the hearing of the ear: but now mine eye seeth thee. Wherefore I abhor myself, and repent in dust and ashes" (Job 42:2-6).

Yet, unbelief, which wants to live on reason alone, is so unreasonable that it wants me to reject God who is the only answer to the great "why" of life, and the only One who can solve the great issues of life for me!

The French author Lavredan, long known as an atheist, when confronted by the horrors of World War I, made this gripping confession:

I laughed at faith and thought myself wise. Finally this laughter became hollow and vain, for I saw France bleeding and mourning. What would become of France if her children did not believe, if her women did not pray? Oh, a people whose

fields are covered with the dead. How difficult it is to remain
an atheist on this national cemetery! I cannot, I cannot. I have
deceived myself and you who have read my book. It was a
delusion, a giddiness, an evil dream. I see death and call for
life. Hands equipped with weapons make death; folded hands
bring life. France, turn back to faith; to forsake God means to
be lost! I do not know whether I shall live tomorrow, but I
must tell my friends, Lavredan is afraid to die an atheist. I am
not afraid of hell, but the thought impresses me, God lives
and you are so far from Him. *Rejoice, my soul, that I have
been permitted to experience the hour when, on my knees, I
can say, I believe, I believe in God.* I believe, I believe—that
word is the matin hymn of humanity. For him who does not
accept it, it will soon be night.

The real tragedy of it all is this: "The fool hath said
IN HIS HEART, *There is no God!"* (Psalms 14:1).

"In his heart"! He has said it not only with his tongue.
How easy that is. With the tongue we speak so many
things: wisdom, foolishness, profanity, cursing, blasphe-
my. The fool has formed his words not only with his lips,
so easily curled in sneers and jeers. Not only with the
shrug of a sophisticated shoulder has he expressed his
unbelief. But "in his heart" he has confessed and said,
There is no God!

In his heart! There's the tragedy—the awful, crushing,
indicting, condemning completion of decision: unbelief
and rejection. For, behavioristic and mechanistic psychology notwithstanding, the heart is the seat of our feelings,
our emotions, our will, our unbelief, and our faith. And
when the denier has said "in his heart" there is no God,
it means that he has confessed that as for himself in spite
of all the evidences to the contrary, he *will* not believe
there is a God. He has made the final choice. He has
spoken the great "I won't!" He has said "No" to God! He
has brought upon himself the separation which carries
with it all the implications of finality and eternity. He is

without God—alone in the world here, alone in the world
to come—all alone!

That is why Scripture calls him a fool. For it is unbelief and only unbelief which separates from God. It is
unbelief which destroys and condemns. It is unbelief
which robs us of life and consigns us to death. For only he
who will not believe shall be damned.

And then swiftly, suddenly, unexpectedly comes death
—death which no man can deny—and then we pass on.
When we awake, as all of us shall, we shall know there is
a God. Surely, certainly, absolutely, conclusively, finally
we shall know. Whether in heaven or in hell we shall
know that. For even the devils know, though their knowledge that God is, now makes them tremble for fear. All
shall know.

The horrible tragedy for unbelievers will be that their
knowledge can now no longer help them. Their separation from the God they denied is now as final as it is
eternal. The woe of their despair is never-ending. There
is no hope in the place they have reached. The gates of
paradise have been shut. The way to God has been lost.
Only hell remains. And it is hell, because it is without
God!

Lynn Harold Hough has painted a horrifying picture
of the consequences for the individual who has not been
taught and does not know the ways that lead to the
righteousness of God.

"You did not tell me," is the title of the indictment he
lets a youth level at unfaithful leaders, leaders who have
led him to believe there is no God.

You were my leaders—at least so I thought,
My impetuous and anxious eyes followed your every gesture.
My undisciplined and passionate ears captured your every
    tone.
You gave me a false world of unreal dreams.
You gave me a dishonest world of impossible hopes.

You robbed me of that bitter antiseptic truth
Which might have saved me when the bombs began to fall.
You were my masters as I tried my wings
In the first flights of my soft, tender mind.
You taught me to be cynical about the great words
By which strong men in all the tragic years
Have become mightier than the ugly foes who beat them down,
Believing in the good which live in God
Above the treachery which disrupts the world.

You taught me to believe that golden days
Can be produced by men whose hearts I thought were golden
   too.
You never told me how the glitter hides
The strange black shining of the serpent's eye.
You never told me that the knife of God
In cutting surgery must take away
The dark malignant growths which whisper coldly of the death
   to come.

You never taught me how to look within
And find the Armageddon surging in my heart of hearts.
And so the Armageddon of the world
Found me a soft and sentimental jellyfish and not a man.

Now I must find the God whom you betrayed,
Now I must find the truth which you made false.
On the land and on the sea and in the furious air
With flaming death explosive day and night,
The moral love which breaks the evil to enthrone the good
And is imperial as hate's whirlwind blows,
Must speak the word you did not know,
Must give me courage in a world you did not understand.

                                   (*The Christian World*—London)

   Is it any wonder the Scriptures call him a *fool* who
says in his heart: There is no God!

            Fool was he who set his hand
            To build his house upon the sand
            For though he raised it up with care

And though he built it trim and tall,
  A thing sublime,
'Twas but a thing stacked up to fall
  At testing time!

Wise was he who took good stock
And built his house upon a rock.
For when a tempest just as wild
As that which wrecked the house on sand
  Assailed the wall
That had a granite place to stand,
  It did not fall.

Build your house and build it high,
Lay its chimney on the sky!
But ere you build it, take a word:
The rain will come, and tempest shock
  And raging flood!
So build your house upon the rock—
  The truth of God!
(Poems from the Parables Foundations—Matt. 7:24, 27
by Lon Woodrum)

Unbelief is a tragic condition and it results when our
wills are set against the living God.

In our hearts there is room for a virtue which is the
opposite of unbelief. Faith can enter there too. And faith,
faith in God, comes as a gift from God.

Before God is lost, shall we not halt in our mad course,
repent of our unbelief, cry out for God's mercy in Jesus
Christ, beg Him that we fall not into the ways of the fool
and with a sin-cursed world say, "There is no God"?
Shall we not confess Him and believe and accept Him as
our God and the Savior of our souls?

Pray God that unbelief may be turned into faith, and
faith into hope and love, so that accepting His Son, Jesus
Christ, as our Savior we may follow Him through life,
and in eternity be with Him who there shall be our God
forevermore.

No one needs to deny God. All can believe and be saved. Indeed, it is God's will that we believe and that we shall be saved. For to each one of us God comes even now, through His Word. He begs us to repent. He pleads for our faith. Through His Spirit He gives us the power to believe. And believing, He gives us the joy of confessing.

> There is a God!
> A God Who rules this universe of ours,
> Even though it is beset by fiendish, hellish powers!
> He over all hath power. "Peace," saith He, "be still."
> Tumultuous elements obey His will.
>
> There is a God!
> Be life's vast changing sceneries dark or fair,
> He bends from heaven to earth and answers prayer!
> Yea, many a time that mighty One divine
> Hath bared His kindly arm and answered mine!
> I know not how He answers. Whether angels keep
> Their silent guard about us whether we wake or sleep,
> And send the news "by wireless" away
> To His great throne of everlasting day;
> Such things indeed no difference make to me—
> I know somehow He hath a way to hear and see!
>
> There is a God!
> And till this mortal flesh of mine shall fall,
> I'll shout His name! I'll listen for His call!
> Then, in that world where prayers and tears shall cease,
> I'll bow before Him shouting, "Alleluia! Peace!"

("There Is a God" by Mary J. Jelphingstine)

Uncertain Sounds
(Doubt)

CHAPTER III

LIFE is a great big questionmark. Every phase of life seems like a riddle, difficult and almost impossible to understand and to solve. We are tempted to question existence itself. And the more we hear the problems of life discussed, the more confused we become.

Men question everything: existence, creation, life, truth, reality, morality, justice, God! From whence came the world? Why are we here? Whither are we all going? A man asked these questions again the other day at a student conference at a great university where I spoke, saying they were the only *real* questions in life after all.

Men come and go. They work feverishly for a short space of time and then they are gone. What is it all about? Is there no reality? Nothing we can cling to? Isn't there anything we can accept? Nothing we can believe? Is there no truth, nothing that is going to last? Must we doubt everything, even life itself?

And what about God, if there be a God? Doesn't He care? Does He know us and see us? Does He see our

struggles, our problems, our failures, grief, and despair?
Does He know the awful tragedy of what is happening to
us and the world now? Doesn't He realize what our sins
are doing to us? Isn't He going to do something to halt
the devastating consequences of our madness? What is the
use of living if He does not care?

What is life itself all about? Is life only a purposeless
insanity, just sheer humbug, a maddening hypocrisy, a
passing show?

Now, where do all these questions come from? From
whence come our doubts and fears?

Certainly not from God! You won't find these doubts
and fears in the garden of paradise and in the hearts of
the innocent man and woman God had created there.
Theirs was a deep and trusting fellowship and communion with each other and with God. No anxious cares,
no dark forebodings. Only peace and joy and complete
happiness. Until Satan came!

No, God did not cause such questions or such doubts
and misgivings.

They came with sin. And the devil, father of all lies,
placed them in the heart of man. They came with the
sin of disobedience when desire caused Adam and Eve to
question the truth of God's Word (Gen. 3:1). Doubt came
with sin. And since that first temptation which brought
Adam and Eve to doubt God and to fall, men everywhere, being all sinners, have had a share in the curse of
the doubting heart.

Men doubt God now as they did then. They doubt His
justice, His providence, His power, and His love. They
doubt truth and wallow in falsehood. They doubt everything, even the distinction between right and wrong.
Above the Bible they place now the Nietzschian philosophy with its amoral position "Beyond Good and Evil."
With it has come the totalitarian ideologies which are
destroying the world today.

Doubt brings on despair. There is nothing the devil wants more than that. When we have learned to doubt, and doubting have thrown overboard every vestige of trust and faith, then there is nothing left but despair. And despair is the awful realization that we have no longer even any hope. To be without hope is to be without God. Then there follows the philosophy of pessimism which says: Well, if we can know nothing for certain, why bother; why bother at all? And the philosophy of hedonism which says: Enjoy whatever you can, and to the full. For tomorrow it all ends; tomorrow we die.

Yes, we die! That is certain after all. We die, and then comes judgment.

Even the idea of judgment does not prevent us from the curse of our doubts. How we despise those who believe! Only simpletons believe—so they say. To believe would be a denial of a right we possess to test everything.

So we insist on our test tubes. Only to discover at last that even test tubes do not solve everything. There are things that can't be drawn into test tubes. Things of the spirit can't. Truth can't. Faith can't. The soul can't. Nor can God. You can't even place any of these things under the microscope. They just can't be examined there. Nor in the laboratories. There comes a time when even the doubter will have to admit that there are things that cannot be proven.

Don't think that we who believe have not had to face the withering winds of questions and doubts. Nor is it true that we have not tested things. But we have discovered that there are other things to be tested, too. We have tested some things which are not generally tested in classrooms or in laboratories. We have tested ourselves. And we have discovered that the truth is not in us—not at all. We have discovered that truth is only in God who is *the* truth.

And so we trust God, trust Him implicitly. We trust God. We believe Him when He speaks. Because in His Word, the Bible, we discover that He has spoken and that His Word is always true. All true. There is no false-hood in God. None at all.

If we look more closely at our doubts—i.e., now espe-cially our religious doubts, or doubts about spiritual realities—they will fall generally and quite naturally into a few rather common categories or classifications. They are doubts which arise as we delve into the realms of natural science and into the philosophy of humanism. We learn to question everything. We discuss skeptically the origin of life. We question the authority of the Bible, the reality of creation, the existence and consequent provident care of God, the divinity of Christ, the possi-bility of His atoning work, the probability of His resur-rection. And as a result of this we deny the supernatural. We reject the miracles and the power to do miracles. We laugh at the idea of sin and the consequences of sin. And denying sin we scoff at the reality of the greatest of all miracles, the miracle of the forgiveness of sin.

Now the Bible is either true or it isn't true. All experi-ence shows that it is true. No truth of the Bible has so far been successfully gainsaid. And even its difficulties are continually being solved and its predictions fulfilled—even in this generation which wants to doubt all.

They scoffed at the idea of creation a few years ago. But now the most advanced scientists demand a creative act and a God upon whom to rest the processes which govern existence. They realize that there are after all only three possibilities which can account for existence: namely, that what we see of the universe must be either eternal, have created itself, or have been created by One who has the power to create. They realize that the uni-verse must have had a beginning. So it could not be eternal. To believe that it created itself demands even greater faith than a faith which acknowledges God as the author of creation. Realizing that there can be no result without a cause they now seem willing to acknowledge God as the author of creation and believe that He made the world and provided the laws which govern the continued existence of the world by the power of His creating and sustaining word.

If I accept God as the Creator, however, I must, if I am to be at all consistent, accept that other Word of His, which goes on to say that I am a sinner and need the Son He gave me as my redeemer and savior. If my God can perform the miracle of creation and preservation, He can and He has performed through His Son Jesus Christ the miracle of atonement, redemption, regeneration, conversion, and justification. For it is only a step from acknowledging all this to acknowledging and accepting the greatest miracle of all—the miracle of the forgiveness of sins through the power of Christ's death and resurrection.

All this rests on the miracle of faith, and I believe, and in believing overcome the doubts of my unbelief. We can never be saved by our quest for a reasonable demonstration of the possibilities of proof anyway. Our reason, even should it prevail, can never save us. It makes at best too many mistakes to be relied on implicitly, or to give us any assurance that by following it we can be saved.

So God has concluded all that pertains to salvation in faith. And faith is the great miracle that saves. It shows us the way to God. It finds this way in God's revealed Word. It rests upon the promises of God. It finds its goal in Jesus Christ. It builds its life upon Christ's merits. It places its confidence in His redeeming work. Its hope is nothing less than Jesus' blood and righteousness. And its expectation is that living our lives for Jesus here, we live and reign with Him in life everlasting in Kingdom Come.

So, the idea of miracle is included in the idea of faith. Even faith is a miracle of God.

To accept the miraculous may seem to be contrary to reason, but it is not for that reason incredulous. Rousseau, the agnostic, once said: "Whoever says that God cannot perform miracles, ought to be in an insane asylum."

And Bettex, in commenting on the unreasonableness of unbelief, says:

> He who does not believe in miracles does not believe in God, but has instead an unreal notion, an impotent, indefinite something to which it were useless to pray, and which is more powerless, even, than all the idols of the heathen: for the heathen felt that a God without miracles would be a chimera that could profit nothing. Such a one, man can neither fear nor love. But men do not want to believe in miracles because they do not want to believe in God; one follows from the other.
>
> *(The Bible, the Word of God* p. 191)

Here is the testimony of a present day scientist:

> Dr. Willard H. Dow, of the Dow Chemical Company, on the occasion of receiving the Chandler Medal for distinguished service in the field of science, delivered an address at Columbia University on May 20, 1943. Excerpts of this address were done into print by General Motors. Among other things, Dr. Dow said: "It is not without significance that the capable scientists of today tend to be devoutly religious, whereas many of those who claimed to be scientists only a generation or two ago took pride in proclaiming themselves as agnostics or atheists, for they could not correlate religion and science. We of today are so much better informed than our fellows of generations ago that we have enough perspective to recognize our insignificance in the divine order."

We believe in God, in a God of power, a God who can do even the impossible. We believe in a God who daily does the miraculous. His greatest miracle is not the miracle of creation, nor the miracle of preservation, nor of direction. God's greatest miracle has always been and is the miracle of regeneration, the power to forgive sins, the power to make a sinner into a saint.

It is impossible to deny the existence of sin. Sin is there even for the doubter. To get rid of sin is a greater task than man has been able to accomplish.

We cannot possibly convert ourselves, or cleanse ourselves, or save ourselves. One who is Himself holy as God is holy must perform this impossible task. His name is Jesus Christ. He has the power to break and destroy the hold of sin. In Him there is redemption, and His righteousness makes possible our sonship with God.

We cannot justify ourselves; but He has the power to justify even the ungodly, when by the Spirit they turn in faith to Him. The power of His forgiving grace can possess us and does. And cleansing us with His shed blood, sin loses its dominion over us, forever and ever. That is the miraculous power we call "the forgiveness of sin."

So we confess our sins and receive the miracle of forgiveness from Him. Not one sin only do we confess, but sin itself. Doubt wants to keep us from confessing sin and repenting it. For if we do, doubt has lost the battle and faith has replaced it. Faith has replaced it, and faith is always the stronger. In Scripture we read that faith is the victory which overcomes even the whole world (I John 5:4).

If we are to doubt at all, we might well learn to doubt ourselves, doubt our knowledge, our wisdom, our cleverness, our philosophy, our psychology, science, education— even our civilization. We may well doubt ourselves and our capacities, doubt everything human, our relationships in life, our ability to achieve, our purposes and our intentions. Doubting ourselves we might have cause for hating ourselves for our failure and conceit and unbelief and inability. It would not be difficult to do this in a day when everything man has accomplished is facing its dissolution and complete destruction.

Only our doubts must not lead us to despair. For despair separates us from God. And we need God, need Him desperately, now and ever. From our doubts we would do well to turn to God. In faith we shall see God and we shall recognize the power which can set us free and the truth which makes life the purposeful existence God wants it to be.

Our task is not to try to run away from our doubts. It is to face our doubts, honestly, frankly, purposefully. Our task is to learn to recognize doubt and to overcome it. Doubt arises not from our abundance of wisdom but from a lack of it. Doubt comes with pride and obstinacy and a rebellious heart. Doubt comes because we have not recognized God, or known His power. Doubt denies the love of God as God reveals it to us in His Word.

By clinging to God's Word we overcome our doubts. The truths and promises of the Word have the power to remove doubt. God's Word will tell us that here we cannot understand everything, certainly not the hidden things of God.

But we can believe and believing we learn the blessings of the trusting heart which accepts what God says and is sure that in due season He will accomplish it all.

The Spirit of God and the truth of His Word will perform the miracle of removing all our doubts. And faith, faith in God and in His Son who redeems us, gives victory and power to live in the truth of the Son of God and to be saved by this truth.

It was in the moment of faith the centurion shed his doubts and cried: "I believe, Lord, help thou mine unbelief."

It was in the moment of final surrender and trust Thomas, the doubting apostle, could see Jesus as his Lord, and cry out in the conviction of a new and great faith: "My Lord and my God!"

The heathen has a hundred thousand gods
    Of brass and stone and clay,
But unto none can he address the words
    "Our Father" when he kneels to pray.
I look on them. And then I look to Him who died on Calvary:
And when I come to make my choice, O Christ,
    How can I choose but Thee!

The skeptic hurls his challenge to the skies,
    And writhes in hells of doubt;
By ridicule and futile reasoning he hopes to wipe God out!
I hear him through. And then I hear a Voice that offers peace
        to me:
And when I come to make my choice, O Christ,
    How can I choose but Thee!

The pagan magnifies a mindless world, and searches there for
        rest,
But he is like an infant tugging at a lifeless mother's breast!
He bids me choose his loveless god, and scorn
    The God who cares for me;
But when I come to make my choice, O Christ,
    How can I choose but Thee.

I know that in myself no power lies to break the chains of sin;
I know that in my utter helplessness I am as other men.
Since I must choose between myself and Him who died on
        Calvary—
Since I must choose between the two, O Christ,
    How can I choose but Thee!

                                    (How Can I Choose But Thee? by Robert Krumly)

The Trumpet Call

We were traveling in southern Germany, in the region of the Bavarian Alps, gloriously beautiful in its distant views with far, far away to the south the jagged, sawtoothed, snowcapped peaks of the Italian Alps rising precipitously and dangerously into clear blue skies. Unbelievably beautiful, too, were the nearer pine forests, well-cultivated farms, red tiled roofs covering contented homes.

Suddenly we knew we were following in the wake of some awful disaster. Huge trees lay uprooted as though some giants had been playing at ten pins. Their bark was stripped from tree trunks and their fine needles carpeted the ground. Homes were in ruins. Crops were gone. Even the grain, the hay, and the grass were utterly destroyed and beaten into the earth as though great armies of men had tramped by leaving the earth desolate and bare. We were traveling in the wake of one of the most devastating hurricanes which had ever visited this section of Germany.

But today those who will can see the awful devastation which in a moment has transformed a pleasant world into a chaos of ruined lives and hopes and ambitions.

Where life itself is a chaos. Where "subterranean forces have torn great fissures in the placid surface of life," where "great winds have blotted out well-trodden paths," and where "inhibitions of all kinds grip the souls of men and they stand still" as in the presence of some terrible catastrophe and do nothing. There is indeed nothing they can do but to do as the desert nomads do after the winds have swept away all traces of their desert roads. They wait for the stars to come out before continuing their journey. Wait, and look up into the heavens, and then when the familiar stars point the way, they go on, knowing the direction is home.

The world is facing chaotic despair. The safe road has been obliterated and lost. And the apparition which has come with our destroyed ideals is the apparition of an abysmal netherworld. Our generation, having played too much with sin, has rediscovered hell, deep down in the human heart and in the social order. Formerly, sin was discussed academically, as Dr. Mackay has observed in a recent book, from which some of these sentences have been culled. That is hardly necessary today. Now it is known practically. Its "spectre stalks across the world, a world which has become converted into a great cemetery of dead values, haunted by restless, ghostly men and women whose spiritual reality has been bleached" and all but destroyed.

Indeed, the contemporary situation, he says, may well be compared to that tremendous vision of Ezekiel, the prophet, in which suddenly he stood before the valley, filled with dead men's bones. You will remember how the voice of God came to him, sounding in the form of a question: "Can these bones live?" But God did not wait for the answer. Before the prophet could speak, God told him to prophesy upon these bones and say: "O ye dry bones, hear the word of the Lord." The prophet spoke. The miracle happened. There was a great shaking and the bones came together, bone to his bone. And then when the dead lay there in the form of lifeless men, the voice of God came again: "Prophesy unto the wind, prophesy, son of man, and say to the wind: Thus saith the Lord God. Come from the four winds, O breath, and breathe upon these slain that they may live." And the creative spirit breathed and an exceeding great army rose from the ground, ready to do the Lord's bidding.

But it was the Spirit of God which breathed the breath of life into these dead bones. And it is the Spirit of the living Christ which today is the only creative hope for a sin-sick world, calling and ever calling those who are dead in unbelief, in trespasses, and in sins to return to the service of God, so that He can use them to save a lost world from itself. If the world is to be saved at all, then it must, as did Ezekiel's dead bones, give heed to the rallying call of Christ.

The trumpet call that sounds over the world today is God's call to all to quit the world's life of sin, to separate ourselves from the sinners of the world, whose sins are now multiplied till the world looks like a valley of dead men's bones, and the dead ready for judgment.

For it is an unbelievably wicked world which confronts this present generation, a world not unlike in its sins the world of ancient Sodom and Gomorrah, of whom we read that their sins were so grievous as to exhaust the mercy of God and make them ready for the swift judgment which destroyed them.

Sin runs rampant today. It is open and unashamed and unafraid. It flaunts its leering face before the representatives of decency, and its mocking, scoffing, scorning, raucous laughter makes even the cynical experience the gooseflesh-horror of oncoming disaster as they watch the passing parade.

Vice has broken the chains that bound it for long and is today doing a rushing business in the restricted neighborhoods of respectability. Its awful sins are no longer the secret knowledge of only the degraded few. Even our high school youth know too often from experience the lustful sins which brought swift disaster upon Nero's Rome. Juvenile delinquency has fallen upon society like an avalanche. Some of our clubs and some of the conventions of those high in business and society are today not widely separated from the debaucheries which make our roadhouses and dancehalls dens of vice and shame. Sex diseases are on a rampaging increase till like great pandemics they are causing despair in our medical circles, making our medical associations cry out in warning as they are doing now through press and radio that men and women who sin must surely die. And, finally, drunkenness and debauchery spreading across our land like the plagues of Egypt.

To add to a situation which overnight has become desperate and ominous, there are robbery and thieving and graft, the daily theme of our newspapers, showing the pass to which we have come. Gangsterism, murder, child-snatching, the terror that stalks by night. Political corruption and official debauchery, crimes which have made of honesty a by-word and a travesty. Paralyzing strikes and strong arm methods on the part both of capital and labor making industry and business all but impossible. Courts that breed injustice and put a price on innocence. Hatred and suspicion, war and rumors of war making national boundaries look like a no-man's land of coming destruction. Sin running rampant, even to raising its clenched fist high against the living God like the statue of Judas Iscariot which they were going to build as a national monument in Soviet Russia a few years ago, because they wanted to put a premium on his betrayal and treachery.

And we haven't even mentioned the sins of unbelief and denial which today like the furies of the damned,

and the horsemen of the apocalypse are galloping across
the frontiers of Christendom bringing with them god-
lessness and hatred and persecution and martyrdom in
measures such as the blood-soaked earth has never experienced before. There was yesterday the uncontrollable
pan-patriotism of ambitious, fascist Italy, which, having
lost whatever faith it had in God, joined in bringing
misery upon a war-mad world. There is the paganized,
racial madness of nazism with its insistence that even in
matters religious the state is supreme and the state is
God. There is the mercilessness of atheistic communism
which declared a few years ago:

> We hate Christians. Even the best of them must be regarded
> as our worst enemies. They preach love to one's neighbor and
> pity, which is contrary to our principles. Christian love is a
> hindrance to the development of the revolution. Down with
> love for one's neighbor. What we want is hatred. We must
> know how to hate, for only at this price can we conquer the
> universe. We have done with kings of the earth; let us deal
> now with kings of the skies. All religions are poison. They
> intoxicate and deaden the mind. A fight to the death must be
> declared upon religion. Our task is to destroy all kinds of
> religion, all kinds of morality.
>
> (Lounatcharski, Commissar of Education, in
> S. S. Times, Nov. 8, 1936)

But fascism and nazism and communism are all of
them in their intentions and purposes religious move-
ments, as Dean Roger Lloyd in his book *Revolutionary
Religion* and Dean F. R. Barry in his book *What Has
Christianity to Say?* have so conclusively revealed. Only
they are not Christian religions. They are wholly anti-
Christian and anti-God. They are the religions of Totalitarianism, and Totalitarianism places the State above
God and in the place of God. In these religions has the
individual been submerged and crushed with all his
rights and privileges and liberties, and conscience and

will and faith have been placed at the disposal of those who govern. And so the world is again made witness to a new form of pagan worship; and fanaticism and hatred and persecution and bloodshed and martyrdom and exile and awful death have become the fashion, putting to utter shame even the worst persecutions the world has ever known, and unleashing upon the world the mad dogs of sin and punishment and murder and calamity, so awful in their intensity and inclusiveness as to make one wonder whether the last days with their woes are not already upon us.

Oh, I think we know what sin is and the consequences of sin.

But the most terrible of all sin is that men seeing what sin is and what sin does still will not believe that they themselves are guilty of sin and guilty before God. They still will not repent and believe. And unbelief is that engulfing valley full of dead men's bones which Ezekiel saw that day, bones which only God can quicken from the dead.

It is this spiritual death—this death while still alive—this curse of sin which darkens a pleasant world—that overwhelms us now; and it is from out of all this wickedness and sin and apostasy God, through His word and through the quickening power of His Spirit, calls us, as He pleads with us to forsake sin, repent of its influence, and follow Him. Shall we not give heed to His calling voice, break away from sinners, and walk out into a new world, a redeemed world—with Him?

Shall it not be the business of Christians everywhere to face the world as it is, bravely denounce it for all its sinning, and then to join in crying out an urgent, insistent, and yet withal loving, entreating, and pleading call that the world give ear to the voice of the living God and repent before judgment comes—repent and be saved?

It is time for repentance if we and our children and

our children's children are to live. It is time that we
turn to God, shun sin in all its destroying influences, believe in Christ and follow Him. It is time that we give
Him the passionate faith of a repentant, believing heart.

And that is the second fact to notice. Christ calls us all
to a passionate faith.

From stricken Europe, and from war-torn areas of the
earth, there come the stories of heroic faith such as shame
us, with our lukewarm profession, to a confession of our
impotence. But no story is more heroic than the one they
tell of Martin Niemoller who has defied the leaders of
Nazism to do their worst; as for him he will serve and believe only the living God. They led him through courts
of treason and back into prison camps. There a prison
chaplain met him one day, this man who is ready to die
for his faith in Christ. "Why are you here?" the chaplain
asked Niemoller. "Why aren't you here?" Niemoller replied without hesitation; and in that reply there is the
difference of eternity, the difference of passionate, endur-
ing, suffering, victorious faith.

I read the other day the confession of one of Norway's
leading poets, whose funeral I attended a few years ago
in Oslo. The great men of his day were there to do him
honor—the king, his court, and members of parliament.
There was no comfort in that funeral, but a hidden despair despite the presence of all these men assembled to
do his dead body honor, and to hail his memory with
flowery words. For a skeptic, an agnostic this poet had
been, and his poetry the poetry of despair. How loud
this despair sounds from the confession of this brief poem
which he wrote:

> I believe in the God whom yet I deny;
> I sometimes pray and sometimes defy!
> I am almost crushed by sin's awful yoke
> And still with Satan's kingdom I joke!

I scoff and blaspheme when the sun shines bright,
But fear God's judgment in the night!
The terrors of hell fill my soul with fright!
I have neither compass, rudder, nor light.

("An Unbeliever's Confession" by Arne Garborg,
Norwegian Author. Translated by B. E. Bergesen)

To these men came with equal insistence the call
to repentance and faith. The one, a great national hero
because of a hero's deeds done during World War I.
The other a national hero, too, because of winged words
spoken to a nation which believed in peace. One lived
for Christ. One for self. One left life without hope. One
has brought hope to a world so desperately in need of
life. He found life in Christ and is ready to die to bring
the life in Christ to others.

There is need for such passionate faith in the world
today. The world has become disillusioned by a generation of compromisers over whose graves tombstones
might well be erected with the inscription: Those who
lie here never had any convictions about anything.

There is need for faith. And a disbelieving world is
crying out for an authority whereon they may erect their
life of faith.

But the authority is here. And it gives to those who
know its claims the conviction of a revolutionary faith, a
faith which changes men, frees them from the shackles
of sin, and failure, and makes them walk out into a new
life, where only men of God dare to go.

The authority is God's holy Word. It has too long been
subject to disuse and misuse and abuse. But in this day
of chaos and despair men and women are again beginning to study its sacred pages, and those who do are
going out to face the world with a new and convincing
changed outlook, and a new and dominating incentive
for action; and this new life is going to change the world.

There is a miracle in this book and it goes by the name

of the forgiveness of sins. There is a central figure in this book and He goes by the name of the Savior of the world. There is a dominating conviction in this book that there is power that will come to all who believe. There is hope in this book and it is called the resurrection and the life. There is life in this book, and it brings life eternal to all who believe. And those who do believe find that it is all true. They have found the great secret that Jesus Christ saves from sin and that He is the friend of sinners. Their lives have been suddenly touched and changed. Convicted themselves and convinced that He can save, they go out with the new and passionate faith of the first Christians, ready and eager if need be to die for their faith in Jesus Christ.

The trumpet call that comes is the call for men and women transformed by faith to transform the world through faith. The call is for men of a passionate faith who will forget all but Jesus Christ who changed them. The call is for your Church and mine to send these men of faith out into a sin-cursed world to preach to sinners the gospel of faith in a saving Christ. For there is in such preachers and in their preaching the eagerness and the power of conviction. And in their glorious faith there is Scripture's promise of victory that can overcome the world. Have we a faith, heroic and passionate enough to set on fire a whole lost world?

But the call is not only for a burning, passionate faith. It is as much for men and women of faith who have a message—a message which will save the world. The call is for this message to be heard now, everywhere—here, in our churches, our cities, our state, our nation, throughout the world. The clock which shall determine the judgment day for the world is ticking on and on, furiously. There is so little time for the message which can save it from itself to be heard. Men are dying, endlessly, hopelessly, despairingly. We must reach them, soon—now.

—before they die. Before night comes. Have we the message to give which saves?

There is only one message. Not the pronouncements of dictators or self-appointed world saviors! Not the endless topics which are debated in houses of congress and parliament. How futile these are in the face of a desperate world need!

There is only one message. It is the message which comes out of the heart of the Bible, the message young and old need and which in spite even of their sophistication they want to hear. How often I have seen and met their eager desire to hear. It is the message about Jesus Christ.

In its essence it contains the testimony Jesus bore to God, and which God gave to Jesus, and the message, if it is a message, must contain this double truth. Jesus Christ has told us all we know about God: Who God is; what God has done for us; about God's holiness, power, and justice. But about His love, too, and mostly about His love. For God's love is wrapped up in His Son, Jesus Christ, and God so loved us that He gave this Son to be our Savior. The message, if it is a message at all, must be a message which includes this.

But the message is a message which God has to give the world about His Son. God tells us that His Son came to redeem us when it became apparent that in no other way could men be redeemed. Obedient unto death Christ fulfilled God's every demand, and then He went the way of the cross to suffer for us the punishment for our disobedience and sin. Dying upon that cross He has atoned for the sins of the world. And raised again with power God tells us, that this Son has the power to quicken us from the death of sin and the death of the body to live and live and live forever. So it is the message about a cross and about an open grave and it has in it power to save the world.

Are you going to give this message to the world? The message about salvation in Jesus Christ? The message of God's love? The message which has in it the dynamic to relate your life to the will of God, so that you live a transformed life for Him? Is it this message which has gripped you? Have you believed this message? Do you believe it now? Have *you* been transformed by it? Are you ready to bring it to a dying world? Are you yourself ready to die that the world may hear it and live? Do you believe it so passionately that there is in you now no peace? Are you burning fiercely with the desire to give this message—so fiercely that night and day there is in you only the flaming desire to share it with others so that they too may believe and live?

The message is sanctified by the cross and the cross tells us that this man who hung there is the Son of God. It was fulfilled on Easter, and Easter tells us of God reconciled with the world.

So there is the call for the message and the message can save the world.

But the message, if it is a message, calls upon all believers to follow in the Master's steps, to fellowship with Christ, always, everywhere. And Christ is God, and Christ is life, and Christ gives life! So there is for all believers the communion of saints, and in this communion we live and fellowship and show a dying world what life in Christ is and what it gives.

To fellowship with Christ, to follow in His steps, is to live, really live. In this life we share His sufferings who died that we might live. In it we share His burning desire to save a world from sin. In it we share His cleansing power as we share His sacrificial service. And in this life with Christ we work and rejoice and love and give and live again. To live is to love—love Him who is our Master, love them whom He has loved before us. To live is to believe on Him and to work for Him for the salvation of the world. And if we live in Him and for Him we shall always rejoice that He gives us the opportunity to serve and to sacrifice. For in serving and sacrificing, in believing and in working we are after all only living the life that is in Him. In Jesus Christ. No wonder the apostle Paul uses that expression so often—one hundred fifty times. For a life in Him is a life blessed by Him, and a million times it may be multiplied as we Christians fellowship with one another in His name—now!

So there is choice in this trumpet call which comes to us today—choice and a life. Life and Christ! Christ and life! And Christ is God. What a life to live, if we live it—with Him!

> We've a story to tell to the nations,
> That shall turn their hearts to the right,
> A story of truth and mercy,
> A story of peace and light,
> A story of peace and light.
>
> We've a song to be sung to the nations,
> That shall lift their hearts to the Lord;
> A song that shall conquer evil
> And shatter the spear and the sword,
> And shatter the spear and the sword.
>
> We've a message to give to the nations,
> That the Lord who reigneth above
> Hath sent us His Son to save us,
> And show us that God is love,
> And show us that God is love.
>
> We've a Savior to show to the nations,
> Who the path of sorrow has trod,
> That all of the world's great peoples
> Might come to the truth of God,
> Might come to the truth of God.

Refrain
For the darkness shall turn to dawning,
And the dawning to noonday bright,
And Christ's great Kingdom shall come on earth,
The Kingdom of Love and Light.

(Colin Sherne)

The Assurance of Faith

The opposite of unbelief is faith. The opposite of doubt is assurance. Faith and assurance both have the same foundation. They rest on the truth of God. They complement each other. For faith is assurance and trust in the promises of God. And assurance is built upon faith in the reliability of God's Word. With faith you pray for assurance. And assurance is a blessing which comes with faith in God. The curse of unbelief is gone for the one who believes. The uncertainties of doubt have been removed for the one who has reached assurance.

Assurance brings with it confidence—not the confidence of complacency and spiritual pride and sufficiency: none of which have any place in a Christian's life. But a confidence that knows that God is the author and giver of life and all that life brings with it. It is the confidence which acknowledges the wisdom of God and His omniscience, which rests trustingly on His guidance and daily care, and which is sure that He leads and that His leading even though it carry us through many a hardship and much suffering, leads surely and safely toward definite goals.

God's goals are sure. And the supreme goal is to find Him as He reveals Himself in His Word here, and find Him as He appears to those who reach the eternal home hereafter.

Men everywhere are on the search for security again —the agelong search which from the disappointments and tragedies and the horrible mistakes of a present hopeless existence is trying to discover a reality which brings with it truth and confidence and peace. Men are on the search for peace again, instead of the chaos and ruin and destruction which have followed in the wake of a philosophy of life which has forgotten God.

Men are on the search for the eternal and for God. For God has been lost and the things of the eternal have all been hopelessly confused and obscured.

Despair is abroad in the world instead of security. Catastrophe instead of prosperity. And war and the rumors of devastating conflict instead of the peace which men must have if they are to live with one another at all.

Peace is gone, and conflict and strife fill the earth. Confidence is gone, and the engines of war rumble across the boundary lines of nations and peoples. Love is gone, and hatred fills the hearts of men. Work is gone, and with it the hopes for a livelihood. Destruction has come and with it famine and pestilence and all the curses which despoil the earth.

And while they search and seek in the face of new and ever more horrible tragedies, men are coming more and more to realize that security is not to be found here after all though a thousand laws be passed to guarantee it. The more they search for security in terms of what this world can give, the more the discovery is made that nothing is sure any more except the very insecurity of life and of existence itself.

Stripped of material security and of the assurances their insecure existence can give, the reality of the spir-

itual and an other-worldly existence is becoming domi-
nant again. And into the lives of all of us there comes the
realization that we have souls and that in our souls we
are responsible to God and with them we must face God.

What about the soul, then? What about God? What
about life, today, tomorrow, hereafter, and in eternity?
But if there is a soul and if there be a God, what then
shall we do about Him? Can we face God? Our souls are
full of sin, they have been disobedient, careless, indifferent, stubborn, conceited, opposed to all God stands
for, is, and expects of us. We are sinners and sin clings
to us, as filthy rags to the beggars we see all about us.

What are we going to do about our sins? Is there help
for sin anywhere? Can there be forgiveness for sin? Can
man appear before a holy and righteous God? Can there
ever be peace with God? God, who has been offended by
our every sin?

Where shall we go with all our misgivings, our ques-
tionings, our fear, our despair? Can we find release from
sin, relief from doubt? Can we find forgiveness, faith, assurance, peace?

I think Whittier, the poet, must have experienced the
conflict which now is gripping us and a lost world, the
day he wrote:

> We search the world for truth; we cull
> The good, the pure, the beautiful
> From graven stone and written scroll,
> From all the flower-fields of the soul;
> And, weary seekers of the best,
> We come back laden from our quest,
> To find that all the sages said
> Is in the Book our mothers read.

There is a place where assurance can be found, and
forgiveness, and faith, and peace with God. God does
promise peace to the troubled, and hope to those who

have begun to think life is a hopeless tragedy. In the book our mothers read, God shows us that there is a reality which stands every test, a reality which transforms existence into life and gives courage to carry on.

The Bible calls this reality "sonship with God," and this sonship is not dependent on the conflicting vicissitudes of life. It may be the possession of sinner or saint: of those who now are experiencing the horrors of war as well as by those whose circumstances bring with them the abundant blessings of God. It may be had by anyone and by all. It is real and sure and lasting. It rests in God who is real and true and everlasting. It comes from God and is a gift from God. It is promised to all who believe what He says. It is obtained through faith in God, faith in the truth that God's promises are faithful and sure, as sure as God is sure and as sure as the certainty that His word is true.

For God is not at all indefinite in His statements as to how we are to achieve certainty and assurance. He has given us sure directions and He is so anxious that we are to obtain the priceless possessions of conviction and assurance that He gives the faith that embraces them without qualification to all who seriously want the sonship with God which makes even faith possible.

Assurance comes as a free gift of God. But there is a progression in faith which to the one who seeks assurance will more and more become self-evident as the truth of God's Word shines into his soul.

In the first place, we must, He says, believe that God exists, that He has made the world and all that the universe contains—we must, as we confess in the first article of our Christian faith, believe that He is the creator of all that is. No one can have the assurance of faith who denies these fundamentals or brings them into question. Listen to God when He speaks: "Through faith we understand that the worlds were framed by the Word

of God, so that the things which are seen were not made
of things which do appear" (Hebrews 11:3; Psalm 33:
6-9).

God wants us to be very sure about this. There must
be no mistake about it. None at all. So He emphasizes it
by even a more definite assertion: "Without faith it is
impossible to please him: for he that cometh to God must
believe that he is, and that he is a rewarder of them that
diligently seek him" (Hebrews 11:6).

So knowledge of God is a first requisite for those who
seek assurance, and faith that God has the power to do
all things and that He has created all things. You cannot
have the assurance of faith if you deny God, deny His
creative power, or bring into question His ability to do
the things He tells us He has done.

In the second place, assurance is built upon the Word
of God and the promises of God. Upon the Word God
has spoken. This Word comes to us as Revelation. God
comes to us from the Other Side where He is God and
always has been God to tell us what we need to know
about Him and His will for us. We could never learn
to know God nor could we know how we shall come to
God unless He reveal all of this to us. He has done this
in His Word. His Word we call the Bible. It comes to
us as His revelation to us, authoritative and final. There
is no mistake in this Revelation—none at all. God's
Word carries in it the proof of its own truth, and this
proof is proof sufficient as it is proof conclusive and
final. "These are written that ye might believe," God
says (John 20:21). And all experience is that studying
His Word we come to believe. We are "born again," says
Peter (I Peter 1:23), "not of corruptible seed, but of in-
corruptible, by the word of God which liveth and abideth
forever."

The Christian believes God's Word. Reading and
studying it, he becomes sure God has spoken through

this Word. The Christian knows from experience that God here reveals His will, and he knows that it is God's will that he shall through this Word find life and salvation.

So, the inspired Word of God becomes the source of knowledge about God as it becomes the source of faith and of our assurance; and assurance comes to us when the Word of God becomes very real through faith.

"It is the Spirit that beareth witness, because the Spirit is truth. . . . He that believeth on the Son of God hath the witness in himself: he that believeth not God hath made him a liar, because he hath not believed in the witness that God hath borne concerning his Son. And the witness is this, that God gave unto us eternal life, and this life is in his Son. He that hath the Son hath the life; he that hath not the Son hath not the life!" (I John 5.) This Word is true. All experience shows that it is. To the Christian believing it, there comes the assurance that God has given him life, and that this life is all wrapped up in the Son of God, his life-giving Savior.

So assurance is built, in the third place, upon the faith that the Bible has a very real message. And the message of the Bible is not only that the God who is revealed there is a God of power and a God of truth. Much more does its message center in this gospel that God is a God of mercy and of love.

When we were still sinners, He gave us His Son, Jesus Christ, to save us from the condemnation and the punishment of our sins. Faith accepts the atoning message of the gospel that there is redemption and salvation in the atoning sacrifice of Jesus. No matter how unreasonable, no matter how seemingly impossible this message, assurance builds upon the absurdity of faith, as Kierkegaard designates it, and accepts and is sure that Jesus has come to be our Savior. It believes that in Jesus Christ there is a full redemption and that "He is the propitiation for

our sins, and not for ours only, but for the sins of all
the world" (I John 2:2).

Assurance relies, in the fourth place, on the miracle
of the forgiveness of sins as the very heart of that mes
sage which comes from God. Assurance rests on this gospel. It believes it and trusts with the reliance of absolute
conviction that God's promises here are certain and final.
He that believes shall *surely* be saved. And, so, sinners
though we be, we bring our sins to the cross of Calvary
knowing that our sin-bearer hangs there and that our sins
are all crucified with Him who has been made sin for us.
They have been nailed to the cross with Him. They are
dead there with Him. They have lost their power over us.
They can condemn us no more. For He died and by His
death He became our justification. His death assures us
of forgiveness. And the miracle of forgiven sin is sealed
for us when He arose from the dead to the glory of God
the Father.

So assurance, Christian assurance, all centers in Christ,
in His atonement, His death, His resurrection. Accepting
Him we become convinced of our release from the condemning power of sin, and with release we are assured of
a sonship which brings with it the certainty of life and
salvation.

Finally, assurance of faith convinces us that we have
life, the life in Christ. We know we are His. We belong to
Him who brought us forgiveness. He gives us this assurance. "The Spirit itself beareth witness with our spirit,
that we are the children of God" (Romans 8:16). And
this is the witness of God: "These things have I written
unto you that believe on the name of the Son of God;
that ye may know that ye have eternal life, and that ye
may believe on the name of the Son of God" (I John
5:13). "I know whom I have believed, and am persuaded
that he is able to keep that which I have committed unto
him against that day" (II Tim. 1:12). "For I am per-

suaded that neither death, nor life, nor angels, nor prin-
cipalities, nor powers, nor things present, nor things to
come, nor height, nor depth, nor any other creature, shall
be able to separate us from the love of God, which is in
Christ Jesus our Lord" (Romans 8:38-39). "I know that
my Redeemer liveth" (Job 19:25).

So, for its assurance, faith looks back to Calvary for the
finished redemption. It looks to the heart of the Bible for
its gospel of forgiveness. It looks, finally, into the heart
of God for a promised hope which is sure and final, the
crowning glory of all faith, resurrection from the dead,
immortality of the soul, and life eternal. It is the glory
of our Christian assurance that this hope will never fail.
It is to be consummated in glory. There both faith and
hope are to be translated into joyous experience, and our
experience shall be the experience of the eternal presence
of God. He who is here the object of our Christian hope
is there in glory even now. He is worshipped there in
glory as the King of glory. There He awaits the coming
home of all those who have been redeemed and have
believed. There He will share His glory with them forevermore.

Faith believes this. Assurance is convinced that it is so.
"Now faith is the substance of things hoped for, the evidence of things not seen" (Hebrews 11:1). It is the
uniqueness of Christian experience that we know it is
all true. To those who have the assurance, faith is
crowned with fortitude and courage and heroic achieve-
ment. Through it, they become great heroes of faith to
do and to die for their Lord. Eagerly they would die for
their faith, as eagerly as did those immortal heroes of the
eleventh chapter of the Book of Hebrews, of whom the
Lord gives testimony that the world was not worthy. For
they became martyrs for their faith and martyrdom
crowned for them their assurance in the immortality of
souls destined for heaven.

Christian assurance, assurance of faith, is not the same as complacency. It is not the same as certainty in this respect that we are so certain of our salvation that there can be no possibility of a fall from grace. The fall from grace is a possibility even earnest Christians must at all times envisage. The Scriptures teach this possibility conclusively. Job was warned by God Himself in no uncertain language. Christ warned even His apostles against any feeling of security as though heaven were already in their possession. Paul cries out: "O wretched man that I am! Who shall deliver me from the body of this death" (Romans 7:24). "I keep under my body, and bring it into subjection: lest that by any means, when I have preached to others I myself should be a castaway" (I Corinthians 9:24). Peter warns: "If the righteous scarcely be saved, where shall the ungodly and the sinner appear?" (I Peter 4:18). "For if after they have escaped the pollutions of the world through the knowledge of the Lord and Savior Jesus Christ they are again entangled therein, and overcome, the latter end is worse with them than at the beginning. For it had been better for them not to have known the way of righteousness, than, after they have known it, to turn from the holy commandment delivered unto them" (II Peter 2:20-21).

A Christian is never complacent nor secure. We "work out our salvation in fear and trembling," as the apostle admonishes. But the Christian who knows what Christian faith is finds comfort in his faith and he is assured by his faith that he is a child of God and an heir of life everlasting.

Assurance is the uniqueness of Christian experience. It is confined exclusively to the Christian religion.

Atheism and agnosticism can give no certitude of truth or pardon or salvation. Deism pushes God afar off. Pantheism denies the divine personality and cannot assure us of forgive-

ness and eternal life. Even natural Theism, though it argue
forever a divine existence, fails to impart actual experience
of God and His gracious attitude toward the children of men.
Only Christianity can do this and does it. Only Christianity
gives an experience that satisfies the deepest needs and longings
of the human soul.

(A Reasonable Faith by Keyser)

Today we need the assurance of Christian faith. It is
the great need of our souls. All our Christian experience
cries out to us even now to cling to this assurance and to
proclaim the gospel which produces it throughout the
sin-smitten and sorrowing world.

O God, this day my empty soul seeks warmth and love,
And in Thy face, resplendent, glows a tenderness
That makes me feel how selfish I have lived this life,
How void of faith, and selfless song, and gentleness.

And as I stand, transfixed in awe, Thy thorn-crowned brow,
Thy nail-scarred hands, Thy pierced feet, Thy wounded side,
Cause me to bow, ashamed once more of human love
That boasts of works, of idle words—yet goes untried.

This soul of mine, seems pitiful compared to Thine—
My highest hopes and deepest needs are earthly things,
I cannot bring a heart so warped and small to Thee
For still about me, dusty selfish want still clings.

Alone and lost I sink, bereft of all once dear,
Yet through the gloom, transcendent light from God's beauty,
Rises above my darkened clouded view, and shines,
Renewing faith, refining paths, love and duty.

Shepherd of men, King of glory, Thy shining face
I now behold, in all Thy bright celestial peace;
Keep ever near, teach me Thy ways, until at last
My soul shall find its holy, sure and sweet release.

("Transcendent Light" by Eva Margaret Sackerson)

The Transcendent Need

So the need of the hour is the need for Christ's gospel. The heart of the gospel is its message of the forgiveness of sins. That is the supreme message of the Bible, and the world's and our great need is to understand this need and be saved by this message.

Forgiveness! The forgiveness of sins!

What a strange doctrine to preach in a world suddenly gone mad! What a gospel to declare to a generation facing the explosive roar of cannons and the nerve-shattering blasting of falling bombs! What a futile message to bring to unnumbered men awaiting each moment the awfulness of a destruction whose horrors must have had their inception in the pits of hell! It seems almost inconceivable that anyone should be persuaded to listen in an age so consumed with the passionate hatreds which fill the hearts of men now.

And still there is one supreme need which comes to us in this hour. It is a need real and heavy with the urgency of eternity. It calls to us who know the remedy to reveal it with all possible haste. There is no other remedy for a world lost in its sin, and perishing because of its own madness.

For the need of the hour is not more guns, more
bombs, more bullets, more tanks, more forts, more planes,
more ships, more bayonets, more men to fight and die,
necessary as all this may be in a time of national emergency. The need of the hour is the need for a cure for
all this insanity and madness and hatred and death, a
cure which can change the hearts of men and make impossible their hatred.

The cure is not death and more death. The cure is not
sin and more sin. The cure is not unbelief and more unbelief. Not hatred and more hatred. The cure is not
denial and more denial.

The cure is God. The cure is faith in God. The cure
is listening to God. The cure is the realization of sin. The
cure is to know that the curse of sin has brought us this
catastrophe which is destroying us now. The cure is that
there is a Life that has come with death, that there is One
who has already died that all may live. The cure is that
dying He who is the Son of God has brought life and the
forgiveness of God. The cure is that in the death of Jesus
Christ there is forgiveness for sins. The cure is that in
Him there is life as He saves us from sin. And those who
believe will hate no more. They will not hate themselves, nor their brothers, nor their fellows, nor their
neighbors, nor others, neither individuals nor peoples,
anywhere. For believing, they will learn to know that all
are brothers as they have been created by God, and
brothers as they have been redeemed by the blood of
God's Son, and brothers as forgiven by God they need
each other to perform together the great purposes of
God. And brothers must live together and work together
for themselves and their fellowmen.

The message of the forgiveness of sins is the supreme
need of the world today. It must be proclaimed so loudly
that its gospel can be heard above the roar of bursting
shells and exploding bombs. The gospel that there is

forgiveness for sin is the central doctrine in all Christianity. It is the preeminent teaching of Holy Scripture. It is the great saving truth of Revelation. All sacred truth converges in its saving gospel. And all men can be saved by it.

Forgiveness of sins is the supreme need, too, of the individual. For the individual is a sinner who desperately needs the forgiveness of sins as he needs desperately to know that he is a sinner in the sight of a holy and righteous God. It is Scripture's verdict that all have sinned and come short of the glory of God. And it is Scripture's ultimatum that only he who repents his sins and believes can be saved.

Unless we understand this need and appreciate that it is sin which causes all the misery which is destroying the world, we will find little assistance in the cures for our ills, of whatever kind they may be, now being offered as panaceas by men and women of high and low degree.

We are not trying to discount the value of panaceas. We are not attempting to deny or discredit the attempts at saving the world from present and future tragedies by the cures offered. There must come out from all this world tragedy a new understanding and appreciation of individual and national and international ills and a constant and earnest consideration of their cure, if we are to be saved from destruction, and if we are to exist at all as a family of nations and as a brotherhood whose direction must be mutual understanding and eventual peace.

But this understanding cannot come about nor can eventual peace and goodwill follow if we are forever going to close our eyes to causes for the ills that beset us. And the ills that beset us can never be appreciated, unless from Scripture we learn to know ourselves and others as what we really are—in the presence of God. Sin has come into the world. Sin is the cause of our ills. Sin separates us from God. And before God we are all sinners.

There can be no forgiveness where sins have not been repented. There can be no faith where repentance has failed to do its work. There can be no assurance of peace with God, unless the gospel of the forgiveness of sins has accomplished its great regenerating and changing mission. And there can be no peace in the world till man has learned that before God we are all sinners at the same time as we are our brothers' keepers.

But the gospel of the forgiveness of sins must presuppose the realization of the existence of sin, the acknowledgment of the awful sinfulness of sin, and the confession that it is sin which is causing the great tragedy of this present hour. Surely our present tragedies must make it apparent that now sin has reached its climax in hatred and violence and the desire to destroy everything God has made.

Too long we have tried to get away from the fact of sin. Too long we have tried to deny the sinfulness of sin.

The philosophy which has become too much a part of popular thought and popular belief denies what our fathers called the "exceeding sinfulness of sin." To the modern, sin, as Dr. W. W. Ayer has put it,

seems but an "inferiority complex" for which one may not be personally responsible and for which one may need psychological treatment more than divine forgiveness. Or sin may be a physical deficiency, they say, and surgery or glandular treatments will overcome it. . . . But these are not God's definitions of sin. With God sin is leprosy of the soul which needs divine cleansing. Sin is moral and spiritual anarchy which needs the judgment of a holy and righteous God. Sin is spiritual insanity which makes the race take its all and go into a far country away from the Father's house and causes people to be satisfied with hogs and husks when there is provision enough, and to spare with God.

It is into the far country of sin the race has wandered today—far, far away from God. And oh, how men are suffering now from their insanity and their madness. Sin is there for everyone to see. And with it have come hatred and passion and violence and conflict and the madness of war and bloodshed and destruction and pestilence and endless fear and despair. Oh, how far, far away into the land of dread and hopelessness and agony and tears men can wander when they leave the Father's house to satisfy the lusts of a sin-cursed heart.

But "there is forgiveness with God that He may be feared." What a change that brings when sin is recognized and repented of and confessed!

A young agnostic drifted aimlessly one day into the quiet peacefulness of a lovely old cemetery in Germany. He came at last to a secluded spot where suddenly he came to a strange resolve. He visited a nearby stonecutter, busy with his chiseling of markers and monuments for the cemetery. Carefully the agnostic ordered a plain, white marker. And on its face he ordered chiseled the one word "Vergebens," "In vain," and the marker placed at once on the quiet spot he had just visited.

Some time later another young man visited the same cemetery and, wandering aimlessly, he came at last upon the lonely spot with its strange marker, left there by the young agnostic who had found neither purpose nor hope in life. But this other young man was a believer, one who had found forgiveness for all his sins in the shed blood of the Redeemer of the world. "Vergebens," "In Vain," he read. What a confession of hopelessness and unforgiven sin!

Then he, too, came to a decision. He, too, found the stonecutter. He, too, ordered a white-faced stone marker placed on the adjoining grave to that of the agnostic. He, too, ordered just one word engraved.

And now men visiting the cemetery find the two graves

and two identical markers, each bearing but a single word inscribed. On the one "Vergebens," "In Vain." On the other "Vergeben," "Forgiven." Two words. Two words with only the difference of a single letter. But that letter has in it the distance of eternity and the distinction of redemption. One of these men found life to be only vanity of vanities, all in vain, everything useless and hopeless. For the other there had come into his soul the great gospel of forgiveness, forgiveness of sins, and he had walked out from the cemetery of death and from the hopeless futility and destruction of sin, out into the light of the presence of God, into the brightness of the forgiving grace of God, into the life which the regenerating power of the gospel of Christ has created, into the fulness of that peace and joy which comes only with the assurance that sins have been forgiven and that God is a God of grace and endless mercy.

The doctrine of the forgiveness of sins is the doctrine of the gospel of Jesus Christ. It rests on the doctrine of objective justification, or the doctrine that Christ through His vicarious atonement has secured reconciliation for the whole world. Its foundation is the doctrine of universal grace, or the doctrine that God earnestly desires the salvation of all men. It builds on the doctrine of salvation by grace alone, or the doctrine that the sinner is saved without any preceding, present, or subsequent human works. It has its cornerstone in the doctrine of the means of grace, or the doctrine that the Word of God and the Sacraments are the gracious means by which God offers and conveys to men the forgiveness of sins and righteousness which Christ has secured by His death. (Cf. Mueller: *Christian Dogmatics*.)

I often think of that incident in the ministry of Dr. George Pentecost, related in a recent book by Dr. Wm. B. Riley, who at Aberdeen, Scotland, one night had concluded a service and was leaving the hall when a ragged, unkempt little lassie followed him. Finally, turning about and facing her, he said:

"What do you want?"

She stood on tiptoe and attempted to whisper in his ear: "I want to get saved."

There was such eagerness in her look and such intensity in her speech as she stood there. He said: "You want to get saved?"

"Ay, sir, I do," was her pathetic reply.

"Why?"

"Because, sir, I am a sinner."

"Who told you you are a sinner?"

"God says so in His Book, and I feel it here," as she laid her little hand on her heart.

"Do you think I can save you?"

Up to this time she had spoken only in whispers, but drawing away from him, her eyes flashing fire, she said in astonished speech:

"No, no, mon; you cannot save me! No mon can save a sinner; Christ and Christ only!"

"But what makes you think He will save you?"

Then with perfect intelligence she replied: "Sir, He died for me."

Thinking to test her a bit more, he said: "He is dead, then, is He?"

Once more the eyes, which had been suffused with tears, flashed indignantly: "No, sir; He is not dead! Mon, did ye not tell us this very night that God raised Him from the dead? Mon, don't fash me; but tell me all about it, and how I can get saved."

Yes, she found the way. She found Him who brings forgiveness, life and salvation—Him who is Himself "the way, the truth, and the life."

Perhaps you read the other day that other incident. Newspapers carried the story. In one of the windows of a large store in a midwestern city was displayed during the

Lenten season a painting of the Christ. Struck by its
beauty many people had stopped to admire it. One late
afternoon a man paused in his progress up the street and
turned so intent a gaze upon the painting that not for
some little time was he aware of a figure pressing closely
to him.

Turning he saw a tiny bit of a lad, looking at the picture before him, then at the man beside him. Then he
explained to the man: "That's Jesus . . . and they killed
Him."

The man slowly said, "Yes," turned and went his way.

But he had not gone far in the crowded street when he
felt a pull at his coat sleeve. Looking down he beheld the
upturned, serious but childish face of his informant
about the painting they had both studied so intently.
Said the boy: "Mister, I forgot to tell you—but He rose
again."

He rose again. There you have the secret of the great
miracle and the power which makes possible for us the
forgiveness of all our sins. He rose again. And in the resurrection the atonement finished for us on Calvary has
become for us the release from the burden of sin itself,
the cleansing power which cleanses from the filth of sin,
and the reconciling power which brings us sonship with
God and the sure hope of life in His name. For He "was
delivered for our offences, and was raised again for our
justification" (Romans 4:25).

It is this gospel the world needs so desperately now. It
has always needed it. It always will. But if the world is
now to be saved from the madness of its self-destruction,
the insanity of its hatreds, the sin of its wars, the tragedy
of its despair, it must now give ear to the only Gospel
that can save, the Gospel that there is salvation in One
who gave Himself for us to redeem us, the Gospel that
all sin can and will be forgiven to those who repent and
believe. The world needs this Gospel now. But the indi-

vidual needs it too. There is none too holy not to be included, none too sinful to be excluded. For Jesus Christ came to call not the righteous but sinners to repentance and faith. And all men, being sinners, still need to be saved.

> He came not to call the righteous,
> That are safe within the fold,
> But He came for the poor lost sinner
> Out in the dark and the cold:
> Those who are weak and helpless,
> Those in the depths of despair,
> They are the ones He is seeking
> And searching for everywhere.
> No matter how low they have fallen,
> Or how deep in sin they have gone,
> He gave His own blood to redeem them,
> And prepared them a heavenly home.
> No, He came not to call the righteous,
> That are safe within the fold,
> But He came for the poor lost sinner
> Out in the dark and the cold.
>
> He came not to call the righteous,
> For them He was not sent:
> But He came for the poor lost sinner,
> To call him to repent.
> And though your sins be as scarlet,
> Or dark with guilt and woe;
> Or though they be red as crimson,
> He will wash you white as snow.
> He came to give hope to the hopeless,
> Whose lives in sin have been spent;
> He died on the cross for the sinner,
> Oh, come to Him now and repent!
> For He came not to call the righteous,
> They are safe within the fold,
> But He seeks the poor lost sinner,
> Out in the dark and the cold.

("The Sinner's Hope" by Catherine Dougell)

This is the entire Gospel—that the world needs forgiveness for its sins now; and that there is forgiveness to
be found in Jesus Christ for the world's sin, and for the
sins of every individual. This is the entire Gospel, that
the Church is here to preach the gospel of forgiveness;
and that where this gospel is preached and believed there
is the communion of saints, the fellowship of forgiven
sinners. This is the entire Gospel that where there is
forgiveness for sin, there there is life and hope and salvation and peace. Hatred is gone. Fear has disappeared.
Men need not kill each other any more. Love has come—
and life—and heaven—and God!

The Transforming Message

THE great paradox of our times is the present world need of the Gospel and the simultaneous inability on the part of the world to recognize that there is such a need.

But it is perhaps stretching the paradox a bit to insist that while the world seems to want the Gospel very little because of any immediate recognizable urgency, and is teaching men to hate the Gospel as never before, there is still nothing men so much need to hear as they do the preaching of the saving Gospel of Jesus Christ. Men are being persecuted for believing and still more for preaching this Gospel now. Suffering and martyrdom are awaiting thousands of those who do.

Still men need this message which is their only escape to hope and existence and freedom and life and salvation. And increasing numbers are flocking to hear wherever the messengers have a real message and preachers a real gospel to preach.

We need the message of the Gospel, the transforming,

saving message of God's grace in Christ Jesus. To be a messenger who can stand before God and preach a gospel which is the Gospel of God is to know that the Gospel is nothing but a *Message,* a message God wants brought to the world.

The Gospel has never been anything else than a message. It can never be anything beyond this. That it is a message is the greatest thing that can be said about the Gospel.

Preachers are called to preach this message. They have no other call than to preach and teach and minister this message.

The Gospel is a message. It is a message God has sent us from the Other Side. It is a message He has to give from the other-world to the this-world. And no one has any possible right to change either its course or its goal.

It is a message from God. And God expects preachers to bring that message to its destination without impairing its intentions or changing its contents. Radio announcers and commentators must pledge themselves under no circumstances to deviate from the scripts that have been accepted for transmission over the air. And no real pastor will dare to tamper with the message God has sent out from eternity for transmission in time to men destined for eternity.

We are to preach this message. We have not been asked to apologize for it, to argue about it, to reason it out, or to prove it. We are to bring it to men, intact. We are to declare that it comes from God. We are to preach it as eternally true. We are to bring it to men, because God has decided to use men to tell this message to other men, man to man, one at a time. The Gospel is, as Kierkegaard has said somewhere, a message from God to the individual, with his personal address on it. Indeed, Kierkegaard's whole emphasis was on the responsibility of the individual to God, and it must be doubly true that

it is the preacher's individual personal responsibility to
be a messenger from God to bring a personal message
from Him to individuals whom He wants to reach and
save.

This does not, of course, preclude the idea of exegetical
and dogmatical development both of the message and of
its intentions as included in the texts that proclaim them.
Scriptural exegesis is not the same as epistemological
argumentation.

The message does not need the props of attestation
the messenger might be able to build beneath it. The
message stands on its own foundation of verity, and it
does so because it comes from God. The message is a
message of divine truth, and it carries with it its own
internal and external evidences of truth.

No soul has ever yet been saved by the *preacher* of the
message except when that preacher was Jesus Christ. But
every saved soul has been saved by the *truth* and the
power of the message. For these come from God. The
message carries in it its own authority and power and
life, and no transforming and saving power can ever be
given the message by a messenger who thinks he needs
to add anything to or subtract anything from the message
God has given him to transmit to the world.

The gospel is a message from God. It has a double
content. It tells us what Jesus Christ has to say about
God, and what God has to tell us about His Son Jesus
Christ. Christ has told us all we know about God. About
His majesty, His power, His righteousness, holiness, and
justice.

But Christ has told us more than this. He has told us
preeminently about the love of God and how this love is
wrapped up in His Son, whom God gave the world, a
ransom for all its sins. He has told us that God so loved
us sinners that He gave us His only begotten Son that
whosoever believeth in Him should not perish but be

saved. The message, if it is a message, must never forget to tell the world this.

But the message is a message from the other side because of what God has to say about His Son, and the work of redemption He has accomplished. Jesus Christ assumed the task that was ours to fulfill but which we, because of our sins, fail in fulfilling. His perfect obedience satisfied the perfect and holy will of Him who created us to be His. His death paid the punishment for sin, for all our defection. His blood is our ransom money. When He died all was finished which God had said must be done to redeem us to God. And in the resurrection of Christ, God revealed that the atonement was a finished atonement, that Christ's work was done, that His Son was God, and that those who believe in Christ's finished atonement are the sons and daughters of God, forever.

So the message must, if it is to be a message from God, always be a message about Good Friday and Easter, about a cross and an open grave, about the death of the Savior and about His resurrection. Because from His atonement there goes power into a lost world to redeem it and win it back to God.

The central figure in the message is Jesus Christ. The central theme, the love of God. The central purpose, the salvation of the world through Christ's atonement. The central miracle, the forgiveness of sins. The central power, regeneration, through the power of God's Spirit. The central means of reaching God's grace, Word and Sacrament. The central goal, sanctification here and the new life it brings; glorification in the other world where God is, glorification and the resurrection and the everlasting life in the eternal presence of God which comes to all who believe the message of Christ's everlasting gospel.

The only business a preacher has is to preach and everlastingly tell his message. And there is the glory of eter-

nity that shines in the countenances of such preachers
who realize they have been sent from God.

A preacher to be a preacher sent by God will always
recognize that he has been sent to preach to a lost world,
lost and despairing, as lost as was Nineveh to which God
sent a message of judgment.

The world is lost and it is lost in spite of itself. It is
lost in spite of its every effort to extricate itself from the
tragedy of its lost condition.

The world is lost in spite of everything it has tried for
its own redemption. It has tried everything: the exalta-
tion of self and of creation; the worship of man and the
worship of things; the glorification of its own thoughts
and ideas and ideologies.

The world is lost in spite of every effort to reason a way
out from the hopelessness of its own existence. It has tried
the speculation of philosophy, the discoveries of science,
the culture of education, the mysticism of its own religions. But the world has failed to discover the way out.
The way to God cannot be discovered any more than
God can be discovered. And all those who have tried to
find God through their own reason and strength have
failed. They will continue to fail.

The only thing man can discover about himself and
about God is that he is himself utterly helpless to save
himself, as helpless as he is to find God.

But the message that the preacher, who is God's
preacher, has to bring is that man's helplessness is God's
great opportunity. And the message of God's opportunity
is that He has come to bring us help in our helplessness
and that our help is all in Him. What we cannot do, cannot possibly do, He has done—in mercy—for us, when He
placed all our helplessness upon His Son, Jesus Christ,
who now brings help and power and life because He is
Himself life, and can give life to all who will believe.

Man can do nothing. God can and has done all. And

our strength is in Christ Jesus who is God come to save man.

This is the message from the other side. And great in the sight of God is the preacher who never forgets to emphasize it.

But the preacher who preaches this message must surely himself believe it. And the message he brings must be preached with the passion and abandon of conviction, else it may fail in the great intentions of God who gives it.

For the preacher there can be no temporizing, none at all. For him the Gospel is true and it must be true. There can in his convictions as in his preaching never be the compromise of the "both-and." His message must be the truth of God. And those listening as he preaches must be brought to face the great "either-or" of accepting or rejecting God.

The Gospel is true. It is the message that comes from Him who is truth. And the preacher preaching it will preach as one who knows it is true, all true. Every word of it. It is true and the power of truth abides in it and emanates from it.

There is power in truth. The power of conviction. There is power in conviction as there is power in truth. And the truth is to be preached with power. Power flows from truth, especially when truth is proclaimed with conviction. The preacher of truth must be a man of truth and a man of deep and abiding conviction. He becomes a man of truth and of deep conviction only by the regenerating and sanctifying operation of the Holy Spirit, and he becomes a preacher of truth when the Holy Spirit is given free course to work through the Word of God whose truth he preaches.

Attention follows with conviction as attention is created by truth. Attention follows with conviction of presentation. And the preacher of truth will need to pray for the fire of conviction so that when he preaches it may be done with the consuming fire of the spirit of conviction. The conviction he must have is the conviction which the "absurdity of faith," as Kierkegaard designates it, brings. For though he knows he is preaching what to natural man is absurd and impossible, the absurdity of faith still possesses the infinite possibility of God to change, transform, regenerate and save immortal souls and return them to Him who once fashioned them after His own similitude and image. The preacher is of course only the messenger who proclaims this saving truth. It is the Holy Spirit who performs the miracle of regeneration.

No, the message does not need the passion of shouting nor the unseemly noise of ranting. It does not need the flailing of hands and the hoarse shouting of those who have no message to preach. But in all a preacher of God does and says there will be the living passion of conviction, and his witnessing will be in the passion of one who has come from the presence of God.

Oh, how weary men's souls are from listening to the empty phrases and the shallow platitudes of those who, pleasing men, have nothing to say! How they revolt against the weak prophets who shout peace, peace, and there is no peace! How they despise the compromisers and those who preach but have no message in their preaching! They are weary from their much listening— weary and full of despair because there is nothing to hear.

But they will listen to the truth, and they will listen to those who have the courage to bring them the message of God's ruth. They will listen, and listening they are overcome by the Gospel of truth.

Where there is a real message, the message of the Gospel of Jesus Christ, there will follow the urgency of decision, decision to accept or reject the proffered Gospel.

If the Gospel is preached with the conviction that it is

the truth, it will bring with it the urgency of decision for or against the truth. For God does not offer salvation without intending that this gift be accepted. While man has the possibility of the rejecting will, it is God's will to so bring to man's soul the urgency of accepting this gospel in the present *now,* that is his, and God is so anxious that the message be accepted, that through it He gives to each individual *the power to accept it, accept* and *be saved.* The preacher has the responsibility through the message to emphasize the urgency of decision, either for life or for eternal separation from God. But again it is God alone who through His Spirit *gives* the power to decide to accept.

So life for preacher and hearer becomes the great moment of decision, and the moment becomes for the individual the great possibility of God. No wonder Karl Barth spends much time on the eternal significance of what he calls "The Moment," and Søren Kierkegaard on what he designates "The Instant." Either expression is but an attempted designation of the eternal significance of that moment when, existentially, the sinner stands before God.

Decision comes when a sinner sees himself as he is "before God." It is the preaching of the Law that convinces man of sin and guilt. But decision "for God" comes when through the preaching of the Gospel a sinner can see that the love of Jesus Christ has been revealed to cover his every sin, and wipe it from God's sight forever.

So decisions for God are made when the power of God's Spirit is released through the message of God's Word. And it is the preacher's privilege and responsibility always to preach this Word.

When decisions for God are made through the mediation of God's Spirit there comes to the heart, before so disillusioned and so full of despair, the light and the hope of the Gospel, and where this light and this hope have entered the heart, there is life, too, and salvation, and joy, and peace, through Jesus Christ our Lord.

The decision to become a follower of Jesus Christ and a child of God is the goal of the Christian message as it is the goal of the gospel of Jesus Christ. And blessed beyond measure is the preacher who in his preaching has no other goal than the exalted goal of the Gospel he preaches.

There is one final factor which should be mentioned if the preacher is to be effective in his preaching. And it becomes such a vital factor both for the preacher and for his preaching because his preaching, as well as he who is the preacher, seems to be so far separated in time from Him who is the center of the message to be preached, and from the event which has given Jesus Christ such saving preeminence both for time and eternity. It is perhaps true that discipleship with Jesus was difficult for the contemporaries of Jesus Christ, because of the familiarity of proximity. But it is also true that the separation of generations of time and the endlessness of space can discourage the spontaneity and the eagerness with which each repetition of the message must be marked.

The message to be wholly adequate and continually effective and satisfying must be preached ever and again with the enthusiasm of that first Easter, with the eternal freshness of spontaneity and contemporaneousness which marked the message of those who in the early dawn of that first Easter had discovered the open grave of Jesus, had met the angels, had heard their amazing declaration, had faced the miracle of the resurrection, and had with their own eyes seen their risen Lord. The eyes of faith must translate for the preacher now the events of that startling day, so that he may, as it were, come running into the world of today with a message as real as the message the women and the disciples brought back from the open grave.

Today's preacher must come to his pulpit each Sunday from the ever new personal experience of Calvary and its central cross, of Joseph of Arimathea's cemetery and its open grave.

For the message of the Gospel is the message of the miracle of Christ's cross and His open grave. It is the glad message that the Christ who died for the sins of the world has been raised again with power, and has by His resurrection become the Savior of all the world. It is the message that God has become reconciled with man and that man can become again a son of God. It is the miracle of the forgiveness of sins which now is ours. It is the good news that, purchased by Christ, we can become children of God and heirs of life. It is the astounding tidings that we who were dead in trespasses and sins now have life in Christ's name.

There is no more astonishing message than this. The most astonishing thing is that it is eternally true. True also for us. That we can believe it and be kept and saved by it.

Can it be at all possible to preach such a message without revealing at least some of that feeling of unbelievable surprise which must have overwhelmed those disciples of long ago who in the early dawn of that first Easter day broke in upon a despairing and disillusioned group of apostles and disciples with the astonishing news: "He is risen! We have seen Him! His grave is empty! He *is* our Savior and Redeemer!"?

To God's preachers there must, if they are to be real messengers from the resurrection glories of that Other Side where Christ is, be daily evidence that they have followed Jesus Christ themselves, have heard Him speak, have listened to His word of forgiveness and peace, and that they come from a presence transcendent in its resurrection glory to tell our lost world that He still is, He still lives, He still loves, He still saves, and that He is only eagerly waiting to receive all those that are His intc the glories of the great *now* of the presence of God.

Then there is a message. Then there will be hearers. Then they who bring the message will be preachers of God. And then their message will have transforming and saving power, power to save a whole world.

Confirmation of the Gospel

CHAPTER VIII

CONFIRMATION of the Gospel!

In New York City there was released some time ago a musical recording called "Fantasia" — which together with its accompanying fantastic screen descriptive and lighting effects has produced revolutionary changes in the whole method of recording and reproducing sound. When you hear this startling innovation in music you feel as though you have never really heard music before. It is Stokowski's Philadelphia Philharmonic Orchestra which is performing. Through the miracle of Stereophonic sound and Fantasound, as *Time Magazine* explained, where the nine separate sound tracks heretofore used to reproduce symphonic music are now re-recorded to three sound tracks with a control track on a negative separate from that of the accompanying picture, a new world in music has evolved, three dimensional and directional in effect, which gives the hearer a profoundly different conception of music from any previous experience. When, fascinated, you listen and almost unbelievingly you watch the sound illustrations, you begin to realize what music is, if one could absorb it in its entire effectiveness, and not only as we have done heretofore, listen only to one or two sound combinations at a time. What makes this new musical experience so revolutionary in its total effect is that stereophonic sound records and reproduces the entire frequency range that the human ear is capable of hearing (20 to 15,000 cycles), with a volume range from the threshold of audibility to the most powerful onslaught the ear can withstand.

The music begins with Johan Sebastian Bach's "Toccata and Fugue," powerful and majestic in its tonal theme. As with so many of Bach's immortal masterpieces the theme is picked up by the string section of the orchestra as it is illustrated with the many variations, which together make the master's music so moving and so appealing. But all the while as the bows of violins, violas and cellos skip about in ethereal grace, you feel you are nevertheless still only skirting the periphery of the thematic content of his music. Suddenly the change comes.

Through the miracle of new sound effects, you are unexpectedly transferred into the very center of the orchestra with strings and reeds and brasses and percussion instruments joining gradually into a great symphony of melody and counterpoint, until at last you feel you are moving along with a pilgrim chorus storming with chant and with chorus, with shouts and hosannas, and alleluias the very gates of heaven itself. You awaken at last as from a trance, with the shouts of victory from angelic hosts sounding in your ears and in your heart. And you are not amazed when you emerge from unforgettable impressions to find your face wet with tears.

You feel that you have heard music for the first time, really. You realize its tremendous power and its overwhelming implications. You begin to understand what celestial choruses will be like when standing before the throne of God they sing the new song.

Perhaps it has taken a long time for some of us to realize what Christianity really is. Too long we have been satisfied to remain in the outer courts of the temple, where only as from a distance we have heard the celestial music sounding always before its altars. We have moved about in the periphery of the communion of saints where faintly we have heard the changed voices of the saints of God. But we have not been drawn into its center where from all sides we hear the exalted strains of the symphony of God which the Bible has named with the designation: the Gospel of Jesus Christ. We have felt a touch or two of its compelling power, but we have known too little of a Gospel which is called the power of God and the wisdom of God and the glory of God. We have not lived and moved and had our very being in the heart of Christianity where continually one experiences its power and is overcome by it.

Some of us can surely remember how in our seminary days, and too long thereafter, we struggled with that section in Dogmatics or Systematic Theology known as "Evidences of God," or the "Doctrine of God." We were quite sure we would be called upon almost immediately to combat unbelief from the unbeliever's sphere and from his natural knowledge of God. So we studied to acquire a ready use of such proofs of God's existence as come from man's own reasoning capacity and which have become variously known as the ontological proof, the cosmological proof, the teleological proof, the moral proof, the historical proof, and the theological proof. We even tried to specialize in history of religion and philosophy of religion and psychology of religion, perhaps in Apologetics and Patristics. With these weapons we went forth to the fray against such formidable enemies of our Christian faith as Atheism, Hylozoism, Materialism, Pantheism, Deism, Pessimism, Atheistic evolution, Theistic evolution, Agnosticism, Positivism, Higher Criticism, Modern Liberalism, and Humanism. We realized only very vaguely that our weapons were made largely of tin, and that our enemies did not wear the formidable armor we thought they did. We have seen most of these philosophies of life, against which we expected to contend, collapse from their own insufficiency without our valiant efforts at counterattack. For theirs was the approach after all of natural theology with its natural knowledge of God, and no man has yet been saved by a knowledge of God gained by reason or speculation or intellect. Quenstedt says: "The natural knowledge of God is not adequate to secure everlasting life, nor has any mortal ever been redeemed, nor can anyone ever be redeemed, by it alone" (Acts 4:12). For natural knowledge embraces at best only the Law of God, and only that in its implication. It does not embrace the Gospel, and only the Gospel of God can save. The Gospel of God comes only with the Revelation of God, and the Revelation of God comes with Holy Scripture.

So the *saving* knowledge of God, through which we obtain eternal life, is, as Chemnitz has said in his Loci *(Loci Theol.* I, 22) "that revealed through the Word, in which God makes known Himself and His will. To this revelation God has bound His church, which knows, worships, and glorifies God only as He has revealed Himself in this Word, so that in this way the true and only Church of God may be distinguished from all heathen religions."

Now at last, as we face a great world tragedy when persecutions and the catacomb experience of primal Christianity are again rapidly becoming the fashion for the saints of God, we have come more and more to realize that the "defense and confirmation of the Gospel" does not come primarily from any of the struggles, no

matter how valiant, which may follow our outward profession of faith. They come from the Gospel itself, with
the Gospel, in the Gospel, and by the Gospel. And in and
with and by and from the Gospel there is that power of
God which alone can convert a soul destined for eternity
and which alone brings hope of a miracle known as the
grace of God, the forgiveness of sins, and the resurrection
and eternal life.

The Gospel does not need the defense of our dialectics,
of our logic, our reasonable words. The Gospel does not
need our apology, nor have we ever been asked to apologize for it, or to excuse it, to argue about it, to reason it
out, or to prove it as one would prove two times two
equals four. It is its own defense and proof. Its defense
is in the truth it always proclaims. And the truth of God
when proclaimed as the Gospel proclaims it is that overpowering message which carries truth with it, and conviction, and conversion, and justification, and sanctification,
and glorification. And the language of truth is best understood when in faith we accept it as the language of God,
through Jesus Christ our Lord.

Defenders of the truth! Yes, surely! We are called to be
that. But the Gospel of God stands without the props of
our attestation and of our verification. It is its own
defense and its own sure foundation of truth which shall
never be ashamed, because it rests securely on the heart
and mercy of God. We have only been called to proclaim
this Gospel. If we do, it will prove itself.

We fear to meet the skeptic or the rationalist. Their
weapons of logic and reason seem so formidable. But we
fail to appreciate that the "skeptic wishes to escape after
all only the burden of human existence, while the rationalist pretends he is omniscient." But "the one finishes in
inertia, the other in titanic heights, while human thinking has the character of an unfinished, burdensome 'Once
More' " (Norborg). They attempt the impossible task of

reasoning in the abstract. But this is, as Kierkegaard has said somewhere, "screaming nonsense." No human being can be found who exists "in abstracto." How this Christian philosopher condemns such inconsistency and with what biting irony he does it when he says: "While the speculating, honorable Mr. Professor explains the whole Universal Process, he has in distraction forgotten what he himself is: that he is a man, a pure and simple human being, not a fantastic three-eighths of a paragraph!" (Norborg: *David F. Swenson, Scholar*, p. 20).

Three-eighths of a paragraph! How can such an incomplete abstraction ever satisfy or save?

I was at breakfast one day not long ago on the long journey from El Paso towards New Orleans. A Catholic priest asked to join me and long we sat there talking about the realities of religion and the sure evidences of God. He told me he had dedicated his life to the spreading of these evidences and for the contention and confirmation of the truth of the existence of God. He reached into his pocket to hand me the sticker on which was inscribed the sentences I am quoting herewith:

> Every Effect has a cause.
> A Series of Effects and Causes Without a
> Beginning is *impossible*.
> Therefore, There Must Be a First Cause
> That Cause We Call *God*.

And then I thought of the words of Paul in Philippians 1:7: "The Defense and the Confirmation of the Gospel," and I felt that here again was one who was building life on three-eighths of a paragraph rather than on the saving truth of the Gospel; because without the confirmation of the Gospel, the defense for the existence of God has no power to convince nor the power to save. None at all!

I came at last to a great military camp, destined soon to become the greatest military camp in our country. One hundred thousand men in training. A whole army corps to be trained in war maneuvers!

Three of our chaplains met me there. How it warmed my soul to be in their presence and to see the consecrated devotion which marked their every task. "Be sure to have me tell you about our atheist," one of them said. Later I heard the story.

Questionnaires had been distributed among the personnel of his entire regiment. Included were questions to officers and men to report to the chaplain religious and denominational preferences. The chaplain studied each completed questionnaire carefully. In a regiment of 1,514 men only two confessed to irreligious convictions, one insisting he was an agnostic, the other an atheist.

At the following regimental services the chaplain reported this surprising conclusion to his questionnaire and then told his regiment of his personal grief that there could be even two men who would not recognize God as the Maker of all things, the Giver of life, the Provider of every good thing, and the One who could save their souls.

After the service a young lieutenant stepped up to the chaplain: "Sir," he said, "I heard what you said about those two men. I am the one who signed himself as the atheist. Now I'd like to argue this with you. I'd like to discuss this matter of religion with you."

"No," the chaplain replied. "I don't argue religion. There's nothing to argue about. You either have it or you don't. You won't get religion, certainly not Christianity, by arguing about it."

"Well, I want to argue," the lieutenant replied. "I've got a lot of arguments that I want you to face."

But the chaplain persisted. He refused to argue, or even to discuss. There was nothing to discuss.

Finally, nonplussed, the lieutenant demanded to know what he meant.

"Well," said the chaplain, "I have nothing to argue but I have a lot to tell. Indeed, God has sent me to tell you and everyone else here what He has to say about Himself, about us, about our need, and about what He in His love has done when we could do nothing to save ourselves. He has had it all recorded in a book. He wants us to tell you what He has said. If you have an hour, I'll be glad to tell you. But I have no time to argue."

The hour was at last reluctantly given, and the chaplain, who understood the great secret of the Gospel, that it carries within it its own message, its defense and confirmation, went on to tell the Gospel as only one who has the believing heart can tell it. Time and again the lieutenant tried to interject: "I'd like to argue that point with you, chaplain." But the chaplain persisted: "No, there's nothing to argue at all, nothing at all."

When finally he had completed the story of God's great love for sinners in Jesus Christ, he picked up a copy of the author's *Service Prayer Book* which had just reached his desk, turned to one of the prayers it contains, and told the lieutenant: "Now, lieutenant, you go to your tent, get down on your knees, and if there is a speck of honesty in your heart you pray that prayer from your heart and ask God to reveal Himself to you as He has in His Gospel, and ask Him to show you the way."

The lieutenant took the book and went home. Some time later the chaplain met him again. What a transforming change he saw written on the officer's face! "You changed my life, chaplain," he cried. "No, you are mistaken, lieutenant. I never changed any man's life." "But you did," he insisted. "No," said the chaplain, "neither your life nor any other man's life have I changed."

"Well, won't you autograph this book, then, chaplain?"

"No, I can't do that either. You say I changed your life. Only God can do that. No, I can't autograph your book."

"Oh, I believe I understand now. Well, God changed my life. God changed my life."

And with tears in his eyes the lieutenant turned again to his chaplain: "Chaplain, won't you autograph this book for me . . . now?"

"Yes, of course, I will, lieutenant. Now that you can and will give God all the glory for your conversion, I'll do much more than that for you."

And now, this atheist who knew all the answers is a humble follower of Jesus Christ and one of the most faithful attendants at the preaching of the Gospel of Jesus Christ in this great camp city. And he knows, as does his chaplain, who is one of our chaplains, the glory of the message of Jesus Christ which in the lives and souls of His followers confirms the truth of His atonement and the glorious power of His resurrection.

The Gospel is its own defense. The Gospel has a message which needs no defense. Its message comes from God, from that Other-Side where God is. It comes to us here, we who are still held by the boundaries of time. It tells us the message which is timeless in quality and which in time prepares those who listen for the day when time shall be no more, when seconds and minutes and hours and days and years shall merge into the timelessness of that era which in the Book of God is called eternity and eternal life. And here and there, here and in the beyond, we shall learn the secret of that message, that it comes from God; and the wisdom of it, that it tells about His Son Jesus Christ; and the glory of it, that it has the power of God to save to the uttermost those who believe it and live in it and work by it and tell it to their fellows everywhere. For believing it and so defending it by their faith they who believe shall soon enough realize the confirmation which comes with faith, that objective reality which is all wrapped up in the grace of God, lived now in the newness of life and in the heroic realism of the communion of saints, which to those who have experienced it comes as an ever new miracle of God.

The defense and confirmation of the Gospel—in this year of our Lord. And the power of it, if we only live in the Gospel and by its glorious message.

The confirmation of the Gospel!

Did you notice, my brother, the picture on the final cover for 1940 of *Time Magazine,* the picture of the Martyr of 1940? Did you notice the final cover picture in this same magazine for 1944? Strange that they should be pictures of martyrs, isn't it? But they are only a composite of all those martyrs who in this new catastrophic age are being called to glorify God in confirmation of the Gospel through suffering and faith and heroic testimony. Did you study their faces? Or did you turn the page quickly for fear their hollowed eyes, their sunken cheeks, their deep furrows, their drawn expression, their evident passion, and great and abiding courage might suddenly condemn you for your own insufficiency of all these confirmations of the Gospel of Jesus Christ? How I revolted against my own sleek appearance, and all that minus quantity of evidences which might in my own countenance reveal a fellowship with Dr. Niemoller's and Bishop Berggrav's intense sufferings! Deep down in the heart, hidden away from too much scrutiny, perhaps, there might be a sharing of the agony of those who now are persecuted for their faith.

But how could I hope for the courage they revealed and which has enabled them to rise up from the horror of years of fantastic terror, from the sadistic cruelties of concentration camps, the loneliness of sin, the despair of the lost, the suffering of the damned, and which recently gave Niemoller the strength to confess before the world and say:

The Lord of the Christian Church is Christ, not Hitler! . . . There is one thing I want to ask of you all! that we give no place to weariness, to capitulation! There are those who would persuade us that the suffering of our Church is a sign that it follows a perverted way. To that we reply confidently that the Apostles have borne witness to the contrary. . . . In their strength let us go forward on the way—in His footsteps —unconcerned with the censure of men, but with the peace of Christ in our hearts and with the praise of God on our lips. So help us, God!

Martyrs of 1940 and 1944! Defenders and Confirmers of the Gospel! Men of the burning heart! Disciples of a suffering Christ! Followers of the Man of Sorrows! How we burn with a passionate desire to share with such as they the graduate degree of saint of God!

It was Søren Kierkegaard, was it not, who contended that "Christianity is earnestness—sincerity," and again, "Christianity is suffering"—those two great subjective realities which after a lifetime of struggle and ceaseless agony finally emerged for him into the objective certainty of "the forgiveness of sins," the "grace of God," and the open door of life everlasting. Does our preaching, does our life give daily evidence that the power of the Gospel has gripped us—the forgiving power, the transforming power, the converting power? And is our life a constant confirmation of that grace of God which goes by the name in this year of our Lord, too, of the Gospel of the full atonement? Has the heart of this Gospel gripped us?

Sometimes I think I catch a glimpse of this convincing testimony when I visit the pastors and chaplains of our Church. Chaplains have faced me these past years, as we have visited together, with a new shining glory in their faces against which neither loneliness nor privation nor hardship nor fatigue can prevail. "Brother," they say to me, "we wouldn't change places with anyone on earth." And I look with amazement at their lonely, bare tent-homes, their primitive places of worship (or none at all), their long hours, their difficult tasks. And I hear the

whine again in my own rebellious heart which too often
complainingly says: "Only, give me some other parish,
another place to work, and I'll show the world what I
can do." Too often we remain in the periphery of Christian spheres of faith and action. We haven't heard the
music of the heart of the gospel, nor its symphonic power.
Nor have we learned the lesson of the passionate heart:

> Oh, you gotta get a glory
>   In the work you do;
> A hallelujah chorus
>   In the heart of you.
> Paint, or tell a story,
>   Sing, or shovel coal,
> But you gotta get a glory,
>   Or the job lacks soul.
>
> O Lord, give me a glory.
>   Is it much to give?
> For you gotta get a glory
>   Or you just don't live!
>
> The Great, whose shining labors
>   Make our pulses throb,
> Were men who got a glory
>   In their daily job.
> The battle might be gory
>   And the odds unfair,
> But the men who got a glory
>   Never knew despair.
>
> O Lord, give me a glory.
>   When all else is gone,
> If you've only got a glory
>   You can still go on!
>
> To those who get a glory
>   It is like the sun,
> And you can see it glowing
>   Through the work they've done.

Oh, fame is transitory,
  Riches fade away,
But when you get a glory
  It is there to stay.

O Lord, give me a glory,
  And a workman's pride
For you gotta get a glory
  Or you're dead inside!

("The Glow Within" by Berton Braley, in the *Sat. Eve. Post.* Copyright by Berton Braley. All rights reserved. Used by permission)

And the gospel of Jesus Christ gives power and glory, now and evermore!

There came into the Chief of Chaplains' office one day a man who said to the Chief: "I've got $150,000.00 to invest in Bibles and Testaments for the boys who are being called to military service. Tell me how best it may be distributed to reach out with the Gospel which saves." And the glory was in his heart!

I called the other day on the widow of a wealthy oil executive who, as I had learned from one of our chaplains, was devoting her fortune to the distribution of free copies of the Testament and the Gospel of John. She had a room in the largest downtown hotel in Dallas, Texas. Surprised, I looked on its narrow confines, its lack of all luxuries so often identified with those rich in this world's goods. Office and home it was for her as she gave her life in confirmation of the promises of the Gospel to the distribution of God's saving Word. We talked long about how best chaplains might reap the benefit of her generosity as they now were called to minister to the sons of America in this emergency. She wanted to speak of the glory of that Word, not the glory of herself or her work. I asked how many copies she had given away. "Oh, only some over a million yet. But don't tell anyone that. Tell them how great and how necessary is the task to be done!"

But I believe hers shall be a crown of glory when one day coming home she shall hear a voice: "Well done! And now come and meet all those who reading that Gospel you distributed so freely have entered with you into eternal life."

How strange, you say, that in this unbelieving age there should everywhere be such confirmation of the Gospel. And I thought I must patch it up when I preached it with my ontological, teleological, and philosophical speculative dialectics—a gospel which always, in and by itself, has its own evidences of truth and its own power to convert a sinner's soul! And which even now is bringing comfort and hope, and life and salvation to countless lost souls!

For the Gospel has in it the transforming power to translate itself objectively and subjectively into the lives of all those who read it and hear it. Its power is revealed in their changed lives as in the sanctification of the communion of saints they daily give evidence of the faith that saves. And the communion of saints has one great reality, the daily forgiveness of sins which the Gospel proclaims. But the forgiveness of sins emerges at last in the lives of those who believe in the new powered life of the Gospel where is ever transcendent the hope of resurrection and life, and the glory of God's everlasting Kingdom.

You say this power is no longer at work in this sophisticated age? That it is backwoods religion which would even dare to preach it?

One weary evening recently I was traveling through Louisiana. Too fatigued from constant travel from one camp to the other to be able to sleep, I sat alone at midnight in the club car paging aimlessly through the magazines which lay scattered about. My eyes fell at last upon an article in a magazine I had never seen before. The title of the article was "Light of the World." Its author, the famous writer, Honoré Willsie Morrow.

I began to read.

What sort of moral training, they ask me, can you give a child today that will be as a rod and a staff through this strange world the automobile is producing? What sort of religion, they ask, will help a child, if any?

They ask this of *me*—of me who have so long wandered over the barren wastes of atheism; of me, who after years of struggling with the moral training of children, go each night to rest with a sense of bafflement or, all too frequently, of failure. Who am I to answer these questions?

What shall I say? Who am I to say? I, a limping figure toiling up the long road.

Then she tells about how in her youth she felt that both God and her mother had failed her. Her sister died. With death came the sense of *fear*. Then in rapid succession scoffing, agnosticism, ridicule of religion, of the idea of God, and finally the cold reality of sophistication.

Suddenly one day the foundations of her unbelief were rudely shaken. She decided she should give the church another chance in her life. For faith, she now realized, could seem no more unreasonable than unbelief.

She had to face the problem of the education and moral training of her adopted children. What was there which could help to make them realize their responsibilities? She found she had no foundation for authority, nothing on which to base her ethical precepts. She found some Sunday school books, Bible stories, and her children seemed thrilled.

But all the while there was the sense of loss, of futility, of utter helplessness to meet the pressing problems of life.

I realized at last that we needed help. . . .

I did some rapid thinking. Why not give the church another chance?

I'd forgotten how beautiful it was. The children were absorbed. The surpliced choir, other children taking part in a program that seemed to join up naturally with the breakfast readings. A whole great building filled with people concerned with the idea of goodness. The hymns! As the choir came in, I realized suddenly of how much that was beautiful I'd been robbing them. "Onward Christian Soldiers," "I'll Be a Pilgrim," "O Mother Dear Jerusalem"—all that glorious music was new to them, and after all, how inexpressibly dear to me, enwrapped in memories of my mother and of the many happy Sundays she had made for us!

And the prayers—suddenly I found myself joining in them with heartfelt sincerity. "We have left undone those things which we ought to have done and we have done those things which we ought not to have done, and there is no health in us." Not my prayers but superb phrases from some contrite heart dead four hundred years, that still could express my sense of failure and of need better than myself.

As I knelt, the enormity of my own stupid narrowness came home to me. . . . Without regard to their divergences of creed, weren't the churches still the strongest, most obvious force at work to lift men's faces from the earth? I deeply desired my children to become a part of the upward march.

Something in the music, in the prayers, touched a spring in me that never before had been touched. All my troubled seeking slid in review before my inner eye. I was tired of the long, long search—for what? . . . Desert and mountains of Arizona . . . the blue hills of Connecticut. . . . We have left undone those things which we ought to have done. . . .

From that Sunday on we have gone regularly to church. The beautiful services are becoming a part of the children's cultural world. They no longer question the authenticity of our family standards, and they are not yet old enough to question those of the church. This is all I know now as to the effect of the church upon them. As to their conduct, what the church will do for that, again, only time will tell.

As for myself, . . . the church, after all these years, seems to fill some need that I cannot diagnose.

Light of the world. King of kings. This I had repudiated. And yet, nearly two thousand years after His crucifixion, I

enter an edifice erected in His name, seeking authority to help
me make my children part and parcel of the process of spiritual
evolution.

And I find it.

And then the morning newspapers carried one day the
story of her passing—she, the great writer, who before her
going had discovered the confirmation of the Gospel:
"We have left undone those things which we ought to
have done." . . . And she found her health and salvation
in the Crucified One whom so long she had repudiated.

Defense of the Gospel. Confirmation of the Gospel! In
this year of our Lord! How the witnesses multiply as we
watch them pass in review! How bold is their profession
and confession of faith who in world shattering tragedies
are finding again Him who never fails, and who has
promised that those whose trust is in Him shall never
be ashamed!

For them there is forgiveness for sins here, and fellowship with Christ, and peace and joy and hope. Daily
there comes for them the constant confirmation of the
Gospel—and its great transforming power. And with renewed courage they press on toward that eternity where
the communion of saints becomes the Kingdom of glory,
and God becomes their God and ours, forevermore,
through Jesus Christ, our Lord.

The Gospel is confirmed in that inner circle of our
holy faith, where Jesus Christ is all in all: Christ, Savior,
Redeemer, Lord, God! It is there the Spirit daily sheds
upon those that are His, His power, His love, His passion
for souls, His desire that we live in it and die by it. How
we need to break through, into the inner courts of Christianity for power and courage and hope for the dark days
ahead.

It was the King of England, was it not, who even that
first Christmas of World War II tried to lead his stricken

people into the holy of holies of this great hope when in the words of Louise Haskins he comforted them:

And I said to the man who stood at the gate of the year: Give me a light that I may tread safely into the unknown! And he replied: Go out into the darkness and put thine hand into the hand of God. That shall be to thee better than light and safer than a known way.

Now Abideth Faith

Yes, I know—that is not the complete statement. Hope and love abide, too, and the greatest of these is love!

But faith comes first. And faith is essential. It is primary, and it is fundamental. Without faith, there can be neither hope nor love—not in the Christian sense. Nor can there be a greater or a greatest. Only where faith exists and where it persists can there be these other virtues. And only then can they prevail.

It is faith men have tried to take away from us. And it is faith that is being attacked now. Violently. Persistently. Mercilessly. It has always been under fire. It always will be. Till faith is translated into vision, into celestial experience. Then love will prevail. Forever and ever.

But now abideth faith. Thank God it still abides. Indeed, there is a resurgence of faith and a rebaptism of conviction, as there is a renewal of appreciation for things Christian. There is a rebirth of faith. Perhaps it has taken a world cataclysm such as that which has so suddenly overwhelmed us to bring it about. For certainly all else has failed as the world itself faces its own disillusionment.

It was Dr. J. Gresham Machen who, almost twenty

years ago, during a great controversy in which he fought
so valiantly for the Christian faith, wrote his really remarkable book, *What Is Faith?* He was at sword's point
with Modernist theology, which so insidiously had
wormed its way into the classrooms and pulpits of Christendom. And he was being ridiculed and maligned for
venturing forth in the battle for fundamental truths of
the Christian faith against the pragmatism of the liberal
school of theologians. Like a prophet he spoke:

We look not for a mere continuation of spiritual conditions
that now exist, but for an outburst of new power; we are seeking in particular to arouse youth from its present uncritical
repetition of current phrases, into some genuine examination
of the basis of life; and we believe that Christianity flourishes
not in darkness, but in the light. A revival of the Christian
religion, we believe, will deliver mankind from its present
bondage, and, like the great revival of the sixteenth century,
will bring liberty to mankind. *Such a revival will be not the
work of man, but the work of the Spirit of God.* But one of the
means which the Spirit will use, we believe, is an awakening
of the intellect. The retrograde, anti-intellectual movement
called Modernism, a movement which really degrades the intellect by excluding it from the sphere of religion, will be
overcome, and thinking will again come to its rights. The
new Reformation . . . will be accompanied by the new Ren-
aissance (p. 18).

And then he presented in the spirit of the honesty of
the Scriptures, the Gospel message of faith, faith in the
grace of God brought to us by the merits of Jesus Christ.
The ground covered is the familiar presentation which
begins with sin and man's fall and proceeds by showing
the Scriptures' way out through repentance, conversion,
or regeneration, justification, sanctification, and glorification. Fearlessly Dr. Machen championed again the central truth of Scripture: "Scripture alone, grace alone, and

faith alone." It was while defending this truth that he
went home to glory.

Strange that one of the best descriptions of Modernism
was that contained in a famous article by Mr. H. L.
Mencken, written on the occasion of the death of Dr. J.
G. Machen. Machen was one of the greatest antagonists
of Modernism in the Church. A few weeks after his death,
in 1927, Mr. Mencken gave to the *Baltimore Evening Sun*
his famous article entitled "Doctor Fundamentalis." In
it occurs the following characterization of the difference
between Modernism and Christianity:

He [Machen] saw clearly that the only effects that could
follow diluting and polluting Christianity in the Modernist
manner would be its complete abandonment and ruin. Either
it was true, or it was not true. If, as he believed, it was true,
then there could be no compromise with persons who sought
to whittle away its essential postulates, however respectable
their motives.

On the one hand they sought to retain membership in the
fellowship of the faithful, but on the other hand they pre-
sumed to repeal and re-enact with amendments the body of
doctrine on which that fellowship rested. In particular, they
essayed to overhaul the Scriptural authority which lay at the
bottom of the whole matter, retaining what coincided with
their private notions and rejecting whatever upset them.

Either it was the Word of God, or it was not the Word of
God, and if it was, then it was equally authoritative in all its
details and had to be accepted or rejected as a whole. No one
was free to mutilate it or to read things into it that were not
there. Machen argued them quite out of court and sent them
scurrying back to their literary and sociological Kaffeeklatsche.

It is my belief, as a friendly neutral in all such high and
ghostly matters, that the body of doctrine known as Modernism
is completely incompatible, not only with anything rationally
describable as Christianity, but also with anything deserving
to pass as religion in general. Religion, if it is to retain any
genuine significance, can never be reduced to a series of sweet

attitudes, possibly to anyone not actually in jail for felony. It is, on the contrary, a corpus of powerful and profound convictions, many of them not open to logical analysis. Its inherent improbabilities are not sources of weakness to it, but of strength. It is potent in a man in proportion as he is willing to reject all overt evidences and accept its fundamental postulates, however unprovable they may be by secular means, as massive and incontrovertible facts.

That, it seems to me, is what the Modernists have done, no doubt with the best intentions in the world. They have tried to get rid of all the logical difficulties of religion and yet preserve a generally pious cast of mind. It is a vain enterprise. What they have left, once they have achieved their imprudent scavenging, is hardly more than a row of hollow platitudes, as empty of psychological force and effect as so many nursery rhymes. They may be good people, and they may even be contented and happy, but they are no more religious than Dr. Einstein.

"Coming from a man like Mr. Mencken, who is not a theologian nor indeed a friend of Christianity, but who is a keen observer of world affairs, this judgment on Modernism deserves a permanent place in our records."

(G. in *The Lutheran Witness*)

At that time Modernism and Liberalism occupied the seats of power in the theological world. And Evolutionism ruled supreme in the classrooms of natural science.

There seemed so little immediate likelihood of deliverance. Faith seemed to be dying, and Christianity was considered to be all but dead. Machen and men like him were laughed out of court or ignored. The twilight of the great apostasy was upon the earth.

And still, only a few years later, the world of thought is startled to see a recognized scholar like Dr. Walter Lowrie step out boldly to declare, in his exhaustive introduction to the philosophy of Søren Kierkegaard, the Danish religious and Christian philosopher:

According to Brandes it was deplorable that Søren Kierkegaard had no appreciation of the great and fruitful thought of his day, such as the progress of human culture, the intellectual conquests of science, the proof of God from nature, the doctrine of political liberalism. He hazards the guess that if Søren Kierkegaard had lived till Darwin's time he would have ridiculed his doctrine. Very likely—but this suspicion *does not seem so dreadful now, when everybody has abandoned that doctrine.* "Kierkegaard neither can nor will understand," says Brandes, "that history of modern literature is identical with its deliverance from the moral and religious conceptions of tradition." In fact, *it was in the twilight of all these gods which Brandes worshipped* that Søren Kierkegaard's position began to be appreciated.

And again:

Evidently Søren Kierkegaard is a dangerous author, and those who wish to stand pat had better not meddle with him. With respect to Christianity especially he has posited sharply the either/or. His exposition of what Christianity essentially is he has made so clear, so uncompromising, and so convincing that every attempt to evade the dilemma is frustrated, every mediating solution, every "this as well as that," rigorously excluded. Søren Kierkegaard is hardly responsible for the fact that the theological liberalism of a generation ago is not *antiquated,* but he is an accomplice, and Harnack's once celebrated essay on "The Essence of Christianity" seems incredibly trivial when one has read Søren Kierkegaard. (Italics mine. Y.)

(Quotations from Lowrie's *Søren Kierkegaard,* pp. 3, 4, 5)

And now, suddenly, unexpectedly, almost unbelievably, Modernism and Liberalism and Evolutionism are in full retreat, a retreat which is taking on every semblance of a rout. Like the retreating Nazis before the victorious Russians, liberalists are tumbling over each other in their frenzied efforts to reestablish themselves, to reinforce their untenable positions, or to retire to new positions of vantage where the haughty dogmatism of

last year has given place to a confused theistic religious
conception which is neither the Modernism of yesteryear, nor the Humanism of yesterday, all the while that
it is as yet not the Christianity of the eternal gospel of
Jesus Christ, either.

The hopeless confusion of modernistic Liberalism into
which yesterday's theology had fallen is perhaps nowhere more clearly revealed than in the illuminating
series of articles which appeared not so long ago in the
columns of *The Christian Century*. Here the editor, who
could never be accused of being conservative or orthodox,
parades a group of greater and lesser lights in today's
religious world and lets them try to square with a radical-
ly changed religious outlook "how their minds have
changed" the past ten years. There you will find such
startling topics as these: "Barth Rethinks Barthianism";
"On the Road"; "From Philosophy to Revelation"; "Ten
Years That Shook My World"; "No Need for Panic";
"It is Belief That Matters."

Some of these writers confess very readily the change
that has come into their thinking on the religious realities of life. Some have gone a long way back on the
road that leads to Christ. Some have reached their
Canossa and stand there waiting for someone, they know
not whom, to open the door of truth. And some there
are who still stubbornly, seemingly against better convictions, and certainly against the evidence of the abiding
quality of Christian faith, persist in their epistemological
approach to Bible interpretation which is leading them
farther and farther away from the truth that saves.

But faith abides. How startlingly true that is. And how
well-founded the conviction that, even though a world
falls into ruin, faith, Christian faith, abides and will
abide! Forever and ever.

It has remained for a world in utter confusion and in
chaotic despair to show us that. And this is one of the

miracles of a day when disaster is coupled with denial, and denial stands face to face again with truth.

Perhaps it was the rediscovery of Søren Kierkegaard and his Christian dialectics which started the avalanche. Perhaps Karl Barth with his emphasis on the transcendent majestic glory of God made his contribution. In any event, there has come renewed incentive for a restudy and a revaluation of fundamental Christian truth: revelation, sin, the person of Christ, justification, sanctification, the Kingdom of God, and the Communion of Saints. And from this study there has emerged a reversal of position and a restatement of opinion which in theology can be classified as nothing short of revolutionary.

No American Reformed theologian has revealed the revolutionary change that has taken place more convincingly, perhaps, than Dr. Edwin Lewis of Drew Theological Seminary. An avowed liberal a few years ago, he has undergone a change in his religious thinking so radical as to startle even himself. Philosophic in his earlier approach, he has now come to see the Christian gospel as revelation, and humbly now he returns from the land of the religious prodigal to set forth *The Faith We Declare* as a ringing challenge to his church and all liberal-minded churches, to proclaim again the faith of the Fathers in a creed in harmony with Christian faith. His Declaration is not in complete harmony with Christian faith as our church confesses it; but it reveals that a transforming change has taken place.

But it is when we turn to Europe, so tragically torn by fratricidal strife and so utterly confused and lost in its newly adopted pagan ideologies, that the startling change in theological thinking becomes most manifest. Here, in the presence of a denial of Christian truth more complete than any other in history, a new and courageous and heroic faith has been in the making, a faith which bears the convincing mark of persecution and

martyrdom. Because of the war, only a part of the story
is known to us.

We are not thinking of Barth or Brunner or Gogarten
or Thurneysen, much as they have influenced the theology of post-war Europe. Human speculation has been
given too much freedom to make their theology stand
the test of eternity.

But we are thinking of two men particularly who
appeared, the one in Switzerland, the other in Germany
just prior to that unhappy country's venture into the
realms of the heathen ideologies which now are threatening it with moral and spiritual, if not political, destruction. Who can read Dr. Adolph Köberle's *The Quest for
Holiness* without discovering again in their true relation
the cardinal doctrines of Scripture: justification and
sanctification—and without wondering at the grace and
mercy of God who again permits these doctrines to shine
into the engulfing darkness of heathendom with such
penetrating clarity and with such regenerating power?
Here you have the central Christian doctrine of forgiveness of sins proclaimed with power and conviction, and
here is set forth with illuminating discrimination the
meaning of a life lived in the forgiveness of sins.

And where in recent times has the nature and character of the Lutheran faith been presented with greater
conviction than has been done by Dr. Herman Sasse in
his book, *Here We Stand,* translated and published in
America just prior to the second world war, as if to proclaim to the world that even though paganism may have
become recognized by governmental decree as the religion of new Germany in its totalitarianism and authori-
tarianism, there still are countless thousands even there
who have now made Luther's confession their own and
are willing to die rather than lose their faith in the
Christ of God's revealed Word.

That such revolutionary changes are at work also in England and Scotland seems evident if one reads a volume such as Canon Roger Lloyd's *Revolutionary Religion,* in which the Canon of Winchester proclaims: that the church's task, in the face of the onrushing scourge of Communism and Fascism, is to "produce Christians and not Christian programs"; that "the Christian revolution comes by conversion rather than by the church's immersion into the secular fields of politics and economics"; that the characteristic activity of the church "lies in worship and evangelism, not in politics"; and, best of all, that its real mission "is to give a man the gospel of Christ."

Striking it is, too, to notice the change that is coming over the Scandinavian countries, officially Lutheran and Christian by virtue of a state religion which, by governmental decree, says, "You are a Christian." Here, too, Modernism held court at the University of Oslo, for instance, only to face through the years a stubborn opponent in the Independent Theological Seminary ("Menighetsfakultetet") . More recently the return to vital Christianity has been more pronounced. It has permeated large sections of the Church of Norway. It is apparent in many of the new theological books which have been marketed. Most apparent is the courageous stand of its house of bishops, and of most of its clergy during the period of enemy occupation.

One of the most promising of the theological writers to appear in a generation was a young parish pastor, Olav Valen-Sendstad. He came to public attention with the publication of a brilliant analytical criticism of Karl Barth, bearing the title, *The Pantheistic Theology of Karl Barth*—a title which describes well the contents of the book. This has been followed by a series of theological volumes, dogmatical in content: *Reconciled with God,*

The Thorn in the Flesh, The Myth about the Free Will, Justified by Faith. Most of these books are conservative, positive. *Justified by Faith,* for instance, presents the doctrine of justification in the approved fashion of conservative Lutheran dogmatics and with a conviction which must be extremely disturbing to a school of thought which has believed that such conservatism had finally been completely outmoded. The passion of Pastor Valen-Sendstad's conviction is indeed the more remarkable since Liberalism has for a generation gone to such pains to undermine true Lutheranism in the State Church of his country. But, as so often happens, the cycle seems to have been completed, and now conservative Lutheranism is again courageously to the fore, heralding its return with one of the most positive presentations of the central doctrine of Christianity which we have read in recent years.

The mind and heart of man may rise up in rebellion against the truths of God's Holy Word, but the gospel and the faith it proclaims still prevail. Kingdoms may fall and the world itself be destroyed, but saving faith in Jesus Christ still abides. Scoffers may laugh and blasphemers revile the Word of God and faith in its promises. God is still God, and faith in His promised grace can never fail. When the darkness from men's sins becomes too great, God parts the overhanging clouds to let His mercy shine through again, and seeing it men discover anew that the age-old truths of His Word are the only guides, after all, which will lead safely through to that experience which is concluded in the forgiving presence of God. There His abundant grace is the all-sufficient saving cure, and His grace is all wrapped up in the redemptive work of His Son Jesus Christ.

The other day I was given a rare privilege. I sat at the bedside of a sick friend and counsellor, for years the leading professor of philosophy at a great university, where he had been my teacher. Helpless and feeble he lay. Gone was the physical strength of former years, but not the strength of mind and soul which had made him the scholar and man he was. In his heart, as I sat there, there dwelt, I knew, a great faith. And it was this common faith that had cemented our friendship. I shall cherish till the end of life the confession of faith he published in a recent book; for to me it is another evidence that "faith abides." Thus did he write:

Even if every other American were an angel, and his conscience pure as driven snow, or if not every American, then at least every American professor of philosophy except myself, it would still hold true of me that I stand in need of a religion of pardon and grace, of a religion which offers and effects a relationship to a divine reality that can reconstruct the integrity of personality. As a child I was told that I needed such a religion, but I did not at first understand this to be so; later I came to understand it. And now at the age of sixty, having spent a life-time in the use of such powers of reflection as I have, and in the exploration of myself through experience, through the nature of my occupation fortunately free from any finite bonds tying me to an institutional loyalty or to a dogmatic adherence, I still know no better than what my mother told me was and is the simple truth. But one thing is certain: No man who approaches the God-idea from any other standpoint than from the standpoint of his own moral imperfection, will ever have occasion to know the height and breadth and depth of the love of God, which passeth all understanding.

Some of us have perhaps lived long enough to have seen and experienced these revolutionary convulsions which have changed the world and can change us. And so we have learned to appreciate that even when the darkness of chaotic despair fills the earth as it does today, faith can still abide and does. Men still come back from their long, fruitless search for selfish satisfaction to the only truth that can satisfy and save. They discover that this truth has been here all the while and that it was they and not truth which changed. At last the hard lesson of life is learned, that "before God" man must, if he is to be God's at all, divest himself of everything that he thought he personally possessed. He must give up "his all," in order that "God's all" may be his instead.

Pastor Valen-Sendstad is a living illustration of this truth. He is now suffering because of his faith the tortures of a German concentration camp in Norway, sacrificing his all that Christ may become all for himself and his countrymen.

So we "give Him our all," in order that "He may give us His all." And "His all" comes to us in Christ Jesus, His Son, who is God's "all-in-all," as He will be our inclusive all when, in the complete bankruptcy of our own sufficiency, we believe in Him and become His, forever and ever.

And so faith in Him abides—and hope, and love, too.

Whom We Believe

THERE were not many evidences of kingly glory, majestic power, or of the trumpets of God proclaiming the triumph of an eternal Kingdom manifested the day Jesus of Nazareth made His entry into Jerusalem. The shouts and acclaim of a few faithful followers, the broken palm branches strewn by women and children, the pitiful spectacle of a humble Nazarene astride the foal of an ass—that is all.

And still only a week later there was the riven tomb, the empty grave, the shining herald angel proclaiming to an astonished world the greatest victory in eternity. And beyond the glories of resurrection morning were the opened gates of heaven, with angels and archangels rushing forth from the throne of God to receive the victor, and tens of thousands of the trumpets of God proclaiming the triumph their risen King had gained over all the hosts of darkness.

How strange it is that the world and we who are of it have such difficulty in recognizing the Christ of the Jerusalem and Calvary road as the King of the glory road! How beyond all comprehension it is that we cannot hear the trumpets of God whose pealing message echoes the triumph that is His and which shall be His in the great forever that is to be! But that is the challenge that meets us, whoever we are, that the victory He has won and the triumph that is His must become real in the soul of each individual as he faces the Christ of God. And in the ears of none of us will the trumpets of God sound their triumph for us until Christ has become God in us.

So then, our times with all their problems which today so sorely oppress us, international and national, moral and social, religious and spiritual, are a testing time after all for the individual. It is a time of decision. The solution to the world's problems lies with the individual insofar as he has met the test. Like the trumpets of God, that message is proclaimed.

To the individual comes the great challenge of decision. And the great challenge that must be faced is the challenge that comes from the last analysis of all our problems, the challenge of decision as regards Christ, who is the very heart of life itself, who determines our relation both to God and to our fellowman.

No one has given the world what the world needs in times like these, unless he has faced the challenge of decision for Christ, whose life and whose teachings solve every real issue of life. The ultimate of worth for the world and the ultimate of service in the world follows with those whose lives are wrapped up in the life of Jesus Christ; who believe on Him passionately as the Christ of God and the Savior of their lost souls; who in faith share the life He lived for us all; and who in this life are willing and glad to walk with Him the Jerusalem Road and the Calvary Road and the Resurrection Road into that newness of life which is called the Glory Road, where the trumpets of God each day sound the victory which has been won by Him and which can be won again by all those who in Him have found the Christ of God.

It was this challenge of decision Pilate, the Roman governor, faced that day Jesus was brought before him to be judged by him. But he knew that day when he faced Jesus that it was not his to judge Jesus. Jesus would ultimately judge him. And every man who has faced the Christ since that day has known some of the meaning of the tragedy which Pilate in the moment of his decision experienced as he faced and failed God.

The Jews that day at the gates of Jerusalem were listening for other trumpets than the trumpets of God. So was Pilate the day he faced Jesus in the court of judgment. Pilate had heard till then only the trumpets of Caesar and the fanfare that was his whenever he stepped out to represent the power of Caesar.

Pilate stood then as always for Rome, Jesus for Israel. Pilate stood for blood and iron and the power of world conquering armies, as do the Caesars of today. Jesus stood for peace and love and mercy. Pilate stood for might. Jesus for right. Pilate stood for bondage. Jesus for justice. Pilate stood for selfishness, Jesus stood for self-sacrifice and service. Pilate stood for unbelief. But Jesus stood for faith in God and for God, as He Himself was and is God.

And these are the forces which ever strive for mastery in the human soul and which determine a soul's ultimate worth in the world and for eternity. Caesar or Christ. The world or God. Unbelief or faith. Satan or the Redeemer. Rejection, or salvation because of Him whom we believe.

Him whom we believe! Lowly was His birth. Humble His parents. Misunderstood His life. Tragic His death. Yet out from it all the only real life in the world was born.

No Caesar entering Rome dragging captive kings at his chariot wheels has known the power or exercised the lordship of that humble Nazarene, who was given a name

above every name. His throne was a cross. Yet from it
He rules the world, even now.

Pilate brings Him forth one day from the judgment
hall that the Jews may learn to pity Him. "Behold the
man," he cries out to them. And then they crucified Him.
His crucifixion was the crime of crimes. They sought to
get rid of Him by His death. But the cross became God's
power of drawing men to Himself through the redemption won for us there. And so His cross became the
victory that shall win a world.

He had no army. He forbade His servants to fight.
Yet He is the conqueror of nations and peoples and before Him the trumpets of God shall sound forevermore.
He denied Himself the use of force and limited His
armor to love. Yet He has drawn multitudes to Himself.
He chose for His weapon the foolishness of preaching,
but by that weapon He has accomplished the one great
revolution in the history of the race. His power is utterly a spiritual power; it has no need of earthly numbers,
wealth or reputation. When He died He left behind Him
a handful of discouraged men hiding in an upper room.
But they went out the strongest of men to conquer a
world in His name.

He called Himself a servant. He was despised, afflicted,
rejected, a man of sorrows and acquainted with grief. But
He was more than kingly in His meekness, more than
royal in His weakness.

A new kind of kingship was His whether in life or in
death. And when we recognize it, we shall discover that
it stands for the only power that is pure, and the only
hope for mankind, lost now and despairing, because it
has lost God. Strong always, His strength was the strength
of Spirit and this was the Spirit of the living God. From
a tempting greater than that ever inflicted upon anyone
else He came back strong because His strength was
placed in God.

He was strong in His hold on nature: and wind and wave, the laws of nature, life and death all did His bidding. The phenomena men call miracles did not seem like miracles when He did them. He only spoke a word, and behold it was so as He said.

He was strong in His hold on men. Follow me! He said. And behold they rose up immediately, left all and followed Him. Whether Matthew or some later disciple, all felt His power. All rose up at His bidding and followed. They followed Him through life and they became the torch-bearers of Christianity. And the same power is at work now, making men leave ease and luxury and the plaudits of men, gladly, eagerly, willingly, to go into a life full of the greatest dangers, hardships, sacrifices, and suffering, to follow wherever He leads. And following each day they win victories for Him, because He goes with them whose life is power and triumph and victory forevermore. He is the same strong Son of God today He always was, everywhere touching with His power the course of events, sifting and lifting empires, leading nations and peoples, guiding even today the destinies of men—whether they recognize it or not making absolutely no difference. How strong He was! How strong He still is!

How courageous He was! Painters and poets have pictured His gentleness and His loving-kindness and His tenderness and His mercy till men sometimes now want to shun Him, as Nietzsche did, and as his Nazi followers are doing today, because they imagine Him weak and effeminate, a woman's and a child's Savior and God. How mistaken they all are! No one was ever more courageous than He! None more heroic! Alone He faced the battle! Men and devils fought to overcome Him. Friends and relatives forsook Him. He forced the devil to His knees. He drove out evil spirits and they begged Him for mercy. He bravely faced, all alone, His bitterest enemies. Even when His disciples begged Him to yield, He set His face "resolutely" to go up to Jerusalem, knowing full well in that hour the awfulness of the suffering and agony and death that awaited Him there. Alone He wrestled with His God in the garden and His bloody sweat attested to the horror of that struggle through which body and soul were passing then.

Though threatened, beaten, scourged, spit upon, and illy treated before the tribunal of the Jews, before high-priests, before Herod, before Pilate, He silently bore their insults and all their indignities. Nailed at last to a criminal's cross, He nevertheless had nothing but a prayer of forgiveness for those who had committed the crime of the ages.

Can you show me a parallel in all history to the example of this remarkable man? And how courageously He faces death! Without fear, without despair, though in agony of body and soul because of the curse of a world's sin whose punishment He was even then expiating, He faces eternity itself, and finally in the calmness of ultimate conviction He closes this chapter of His life with the prayer of complete trust: "Father, into thy hand I commend my spirit." And having spoken, He of His own will bows down His head into death and Himself gives up the ghost. How courageous He was!

How pure, how stainless, how sinless He was! Pilate could find no flaw in Him, though he tried ever and ever so hard. Again and again he faced the mob with this convincing testimony: "I find in him no guilt at all!" The Jews with their leaders could find no fault in Him. They had to stoop to trumped-up charges when demanding His death, charges so absurd that even heathen Pilate could pay no attention to them. No one else has ever been able to find a fault or a sin in the life and character of Jesus. Not one of the atheists or scoffers or deniers who have ever lived have been able to discover a single sin in Jesus. And so even Rousseau, before whose sarcophagus I stood one day down in the crypt of the great Pantheon in Paris, was moved to say, even in spite of his agnosticism: "Can it be possible that the sacred personage whose history the Scriptures contain should be a mere man? Where is the man, where the philosopher, who could so live and so die without weakness and without ostentation? If Socrates lived and died like a philosopher, Jesus lived and died like a God!"

Jesus is the only sinless character in all history. He calls a world to repentance, but He needs no repentance Himself. He calls every individual in the world to conversion, but He needs no conversion Himself. He is pure enough to make others pure. He is divine, He is God, and dying He takes away the sin of all the world. He is the holy God and so can grant forgiveness to all who believe. How pure, how stainless, how sinless He was!

How loving He was! He lays His hands on little children who crowd about Him, blessing them. The sick find in Him a loving, sympathetic, healing physician who heals their every ill. He lavished His love on the obscurest lives. To sinners gone astray, He was always the loving Savior calling them back from their sins. And to me it has always seemed such a gloriously beautiful picture, the picture of the Savior of mankind face to face with the woman who till this day is still called a sinner. They dragged her from her life of shame to be flung at last before Him who till this day is called the friend of sinners. And then He heard her accusers demand that He join in punishing her as the law of Moses prescribed. I look at Him. Quietly, without a word, He bends down to write something, I know not what, into the dust of the earth. Then without looking up, He speaks calmly: "Let him who is without sin among you cast the first stone." I see the miracle happening, the same miracle which would happen with us if we only for once could be honest with ourselves. They hurry out, beginning with the eldest, continuing even to the youngest, until at last, when He looks up, Jesus finds Himself all alone with this woman. "Where are these thine accusers?" He says to her. Then with a heart broken beneath the crushing burden of her sins which in the presence of her God she knows she is guilty of, she cries out her fears and her hopes: "There is no one to accuse me longer, Lord." And she hears a word, which cleanses and gives her peace, a word which I too pray I may hear till sin is no more: "Neither do I condemn thee; go thy way, and sin no more!"

A comfort to the comfortless and despairing, He always went about doing good. He loved Peter, though he denied Him. He loved Judas, though he betrayed Him. He loved His enemies, even though they spit on Him, scoffed at Him and crucified Him at last. He died to show men the greatness of His love for men and to save men.

Isn't that the greatest evidence of love? Isn't God like that? And must not Jesus be God, to love us like that?

Who then is this man in whom we are to believe, whom we do believe?

He was no scholar, and yet He alone in the moral and spiritual sphere challenges the students and leaders of thought everywhere in the world even today. He was no writer. He never left a page of written word. And still His book is called The Book of books, and today, centuries after His death, it goes out in more than one thousand tongues to proclaim to all mankind the only message that can save. Only about three years in public life, His life is the greatest life ever lived in the history of mankind or of eternity. He was no philosopher, and still the world's greatest philosophers, men like Kierkegaard, spend a lifetime in bringing to the attention of the thinkers of all the world the philosophy of life which is His and which can still change a lost world.

He was no artist, and still the greatest artists of the world have lavished their art to picture Him who is the goal of all life. He was no architect, and still the masterpieces of architecture, the great cathedrals of Christendom, have been designed only to portray and perpetuate the teachings He gave the world. He was no musician and still the master composers of all time have written their glorious symphonies and stirring oratorios in order that orchestras and choirs might forever reach the heart of sinner and saint with harmonies which tell the soul of music that shall be heard by the redeemed in that better world where He dwells.

He was no poet, and yet the world's greatest poets have been stirred by Him to write their winged rhymes and phrases. He inspires a Milton, a Browning, a Tennyson, and countless others to undying fame. He was no social reformer, and still He inspires and rouses the social conscience of the ages with His principles of social justice. He was no physician and still He heals mankind in all ages and even today through His representatives He goes out to heal the broken and maimed and wounded and suffering and starving and dying in that great human tragedy we call our present world. He had no wife, no children, no family, no home to protect and love. And still woman's full emancipation came from Him; He has taught us the meaning of home and family; He still reaches out His arms to receive the little ones and to bless them. He has taught us what love is and He has shown us a world full of people like us whom we are to love as we love ourselves, love as He first loved us to save us all.

You still ask me who this Man is whose life and whose death have claimed us, body and soul, whom we believe, "whose we are and whom we serve"? Who can He be but God, Lord of our life and Savior of our soul? Can you find anyone more like God than is He; anyone stronger, more courageous, more pure, more sinless, more loving, more saving, more divine than is He? Isn't He God? Isn't He the One who can save us to the uttermost, who can regenerate us, who can make us His chosen people to help regenerate a lost world?

Has anyone been able to tell you more about God than has He? About the love of God? How to find God when we had lost Him?

Has anyone told you more about yourself, about the meaning and purpose of life?

Has anyone given you more lofty precepts on morality, how we shall live: No hatred, but love; no sin, but holiness; no lust or evil desire, but purity and chastity; no selfishness, but service; nothing of self, everything for others and for God?

Has anyone done more to save than He who dies on the cross for you? How can He be anything but God! And how can He who gives the power to live such lives as He demands be anything less than the Savior of the world, Himself the One He claims He is, the Redeemer of the lost, King of kings, Lord over all, forever.

Shall we not follow Him and claim Him and hail Him? If we do, even we can even now, when we listen, hear the sound of the trumpets of God as they peal forth on the Jerusalem Road and the Calvary Road which is our road, the victory of the Glory Road which is His Road. And His road shall be ours, when we see Him in that everlasting Kingdom which is His now and which shall be ours when in the fulness of time we see Him face to face.

Oh, how the angels shout their hosannas before Him, the Lamb of God exalted to sit on the throne of glory forever! How the trumpets of God sound His victory, and echo and re-echo the triumph that is His. Through the corridors of heaven the trumpets sound even now. Trumpets of God! Trumpets of God! Trumpets of God!

How we long to hear your sound as you hail our Christ

and our God! "For the Son of God, Jesus Christ, who was preached among you by us . . . was not yea and nay, but in him was yea. For all the promises of God in him are yea, and in him Amen, unto the glory of God" (II Corinthians 1:19-20). And we believe these promises and we believe in Him, our Savior, with all our heart forever.

When God sought a king for His people of old,
He went to the fields to find him;
A shepherd was he, with his crook and his lute
And a following flock behind him.

O love of the sheep, O joy of the lute,
And the sling and the stone for the battle!
A shepherd was King; the giant was naught
And the enemy driven like cattle.

When God looked to tell of His good will to men,
And the Shepherd King's Son whom He gave them;
To shepherds, made meek a'caring for sheep,
He told of a Christ sent to save them.

O love of the sheep, O watch in the night,
And the glory, the message, the choir,
'Twas shepherds who saw their King in the straw
And returned with their hearts all on fire.

When Christ thought to tell of His love to the world
He said to the throng before Him;
"The Good Shepherd giveth His life for the sheep"—
And away to the cross they bore Him.

O love of the sheep, O blood sweat of prayer,
O Man on the cross, God-forsaken!
A Shepherd has gone to defend all alone
The sheepfold by death overtaken.

When God sought a King for His people, for aye,
He went to the grave to find Him;
And a Shepherd came back, Death dead in his grasp,
And a following flock behind Him.

O love of the sheep, O life from the dead,
O strength of the faint and the fearing!
A Shepherd is King, and His Kingdom will come,
And the day of His coming is nearing!

("A Song of the Shepherd" by Joseph Addison Richards)

The Urgent Now

I LISTENED the other day to a great radio program. Four of America's leading personalities in their particular fields were attempting to answer the question at issue: "What is America's greatest need today?" Three of them suggested solutions which have long since been forgotten by those who listened in. The fourth, the president of New York University, launched at once into a reply which brought his great audience to their feet as they applauded enthusiastically, a reply which, I am sure, thrilled his great radio audience as it did us, when unequivocally he declared: "America's greatest need today is a rebaptism of religion. And I did not formerly think so," he continued, "but I know it now."

I attended a national convention the other day of representatives of an organization of national significance. The mayor of a great city addressed us. The distinguished son of one of America's great presidents did likewise. Leading representatives of governmental life, generals and departmental chiefs, were there to speak to us. All of them laid bare their souls as they cried out to bring religion back to America and America back to God!

I read one day the editorial comment in the syndicated

Saturday column of the late Bishop James E. Freeman of Washington. He spoke of the lowered moral standards of the nation and the dangers these lowered standards are bringing to our national life. And then he said:

Something must be done, and done quickly, to arrest a condition that is threatening and dangerous. We have built up systems that rest themselves in fictitious values; we have made the stock tape a determining factor in our economic order; we have parted company with many of the time-honored and wholesome ways in our domestic and social life; we have exalted wealth above culture and have abandoned those moral and spiritual standards that were the strong footing-stones of our dealings one with another. . . . One of the primary causes of our lowered estate is a marked loss of moral values, a loss that affects definitely and vitally every phase of our life. . . . The something we are short of today is moral character, or to put it in more understandable terms, it is religion.

Some time ago the International Council of Religious Education met in annual convention. With startling passion its Executive Secretary, Dr. Roy Ross, confronted the Council and declared that the spiritually illiterate young people of today are a greater peril to democracy than all the isms of Europe, and that an effort to confront young people with the message of Christianity must be the chief objective of the Council. For "America's greatest array of pagan youth is democracy's greatest peril," he cried.

No democracy can be secure where paganism again takes root and dominates the life of a nation. No democracy can indeed exist where its people forget God. Russia introduced atheism and taught its youth to hate God. But soon they discovered that no life was secure there any longer. For hating God they learned to hate each other. When hatred reigns supreme, peace and security are virtues long since forgotten and no man can feel safe where these passions hold sway. Now in the exigencies of war, they are announcing a return to freedom of religious worship again.

They have reintroduced pagan worship into Luther's Germany where once the light of the gospel shone brightly. Together with pagan ideologies and pagan worship, pagan ideas of the cheapness and the worthlessness of human life have replaced the gospel idea of its eternal value in the eyes of a merciful God. And now concentration camps and suspicion and fear and hatred and murder and war have all but wiped out the freedom which Christianity proclaims.

And we in America are not learning by their horrible example. We comforted ourselves a few years ago with the doubtful comfort that 40,000,000 of our people claimed affiliation with some church. We tried to forget that more than 60,000,000 boasted that they never saw the inside of any church. But now statistics recently released have given the startling information that the unchurched number has been increased to 70,000,000. And what is infinitely more tragic, this number is increasing rapidly with each passing day and the unchurched and unsaved are now hurrying towards the 80,000,000 mark. In other words, of every three people you meet on the street, two will tell you they have nothing to do with any religion of any kind. And the other one may, for all we know, in the religion he claims, be so far divorced from the one true God, that God would never recognize him as belonging to Him at all. Not at all!

Is it any wonder that thinking men and women who love America and what it stands for are alarmed and disturbed about our uncertain tomorrow?

To a minister who visited him, President Coolidge said: "I sit at my desk day after day worrying myself sick over our country. What are we coming to, this wave of lawlessness and crime? Dr. Booth, do you know what is the matter with this country? We have forgotten God. He seems to have gone out of our public life, and our personal life. If this nation is to be saved we must get back to the ideals and traditions which went into the making of Vermont and New England. Dr. Booth, go back and preach the Gospel. That is what I say to every minister who comes to me. Go back and preach the Gospel!"

But it is this America and this unbelieving world we must reclaim now. If it is to be reclaimed at all, there is only One who can reclaim it, even Jesus Christ our Lord. And our supreme concern must therefore be to have Him and His Gospel preached to America, preached to young and old—but especially to the young—preached with power and conviction by men who have been set on fire with the consuming passion of the regenerating power of the Gospel of Jesus Christ.

There is a message which America needs to hear and to hear now. It is the transforming message which runs counter to all the prevailing philosophies and present ideologies of life. It is the revolutionary message (Titus 2:14) that "the grace of God that bringeth salvation hath appeared to all men, teaching us that, denying ungodliness and worldly lusts, we should live soberly, righteously, and godly in this present world." It is the challenging message, that we should constantly live in the forward look of that blessed hope of the glorious appearing again of our great God and our Savior, Jesus Christ. It is the converting message that Christ gave Himself for us, that He might redeem us from all iniquity. It is the convicting message that there was purpose in the atoning work of the Redeemer.

For it was to purify unto Himself a peculiar people, always zealous of good works, that He died on the cross. He came to change us and refashion us, to make a generation of sinners into a generation of saints, a nation of unrighteous and evil-minded people into a people among whom righteousness is exalted and peace and the deeds of godly men always prevail. He came to make us Christians, and as Christians our one daily task is to "live Christ," "live Christ now!"

Living Christianity is a life where the double standard of self-denial and Christlike living constantly prevail. Where Christ is lived, really lived in the daily lives of His followers, there ungodliness and all worldly lusts will be denied and fought against and conquered in His name, that those who live in His name will constantly live their lives, too, in sobriety and righteousness and true godliness and piety.

How these virtues are needed in America and in the world today! And how far men have gotten away from all these noble practices, the pursuit of which exalts a nation and brings blessing to its people!

We have been part of a generation which thought it could exist without God. We thought we could live even though God was not in any of our ways. We thought we could prosper, even though we never asked God for a blessing. We thought we could be strong, even though we sought not our strength in the Lord.

How we have been disillusioned! How quickly did our feet run to disaster! How utterly have we been broken in the chaotic despair which has followed all our godless ways!

All over the world men have been sowing the seeds of unbelief and rebellion, and fear, and suspicion, and hatred, and violence, and unbridled passion. And we have forgotten that what a man sows that shall he also reap.

Long long ago, so long ago that men now have all but forgotten it, one of the friends of Job, the patriarch, came to remind him, who was a man of God: "Even as I have seen, they that plow iniquity, and sow wickedness, reap the same. By the blast of God they perish, and by the breath of his nostrils are they consumed" (Job 4:8-9).

For you cannot sow ungodliness and reap godliness. You cannot sow worldly lusts and reap pleasures of body and soul that last. You cannot sow sin and reap sinlessness.

You cannot sow intemperance and reap sobriety. You cannot sow immorality and reap purity. You cannot sow hatred and reap love. You cannot sow suspicion and reap goodwill. You cannot sow strife and contention and rebellion and revolution and aggressor wars and reap security and prosperity and progress and national and international understanding and peace. You cannot sow unbelief and reap faith in a provident and merciful and loving and saving God.

So the trumpet call and the insistent cry comes to us who belong to an America and to a world desperately in need of reclamation and salvation, to live, not to exist, but to *live* as men and women of God, to live in God as His children each day; to live soberly and righteously and godly, forsaking all iniquity; purifying and sanctifying ourselves each day, always recognizing that all who are Christ's and all who would live in Christ Jesus, are all a peculiar, a set-apart people, a chosen priesthood, a communion of saints. And all of us, everywhere and every place, we are all called to be constantly zealous of good works so that anyone may recognize us as belonging to God, and say as they see us: There is a man, there is a woman, who of a truth is a child of God.

And only then do we live Christ!

Thank God, the call to the Christ-life which so insistently and so earnestly is sounded to this generation of youthful Americans, has not been sounded in vain. Not in centuries has there been a more startling response. Not in generations has there been a greater eagerness to hear, and in hearing a greater willingness to heed the call and to dedicate their twice-born lives to the service of Christ who calls. Thousands have responded and said:

Savior! I follow on, guided by Thee,
Seeing not yet the hand that leadeth me;
Hushed be my heart and still,
Fear I no further ill;
Only to meet Thy will, my will shall be.

Riven the rock for me, thirst to relieve,
Manna from heaven falls fresh ev'ry eve;
Never a want severe
Causeth my eye a tear,
But Thou dost whisper near, "Only believe!"

Savior! I long to walk closer with Thee,
Led by Thy guiding hand, ever to be;
Constantly near Thy side,
Quickened and purified,
Living for Him who died, freely for me!

(S. C. Robinson)

A college bulletin of a few years ago and still widely circulated, quotes a group of outstanding college men on their Christian faith. Most of them have gained fame at college both in athletics and in scholarship or in their professions.

Christ came into my life, completely changing and transforming it. He gave me a purpose, a reason and a *burning desire* to live for Him so that all things I do might be to His honor and glory. (Henry Wilder, Iowa State.)

I have found the most challenging, and the only eternally worthwhile life for myself to be that lived in and for Christ. For I am not my own, but I am bought with a price—bought with the precious blood of the Lord Jesus Christ. (Marianna Conde Slocum, Wilson College.)

Living according to my own intelligence and by my own power resulted in misery, but living by faith in Christ Jesus, through His power, and according to God's Word, is joy and peace. (Coach Joseph L. Fleming, Los Angeles City College.)

Jesus Christ is my Savior, Friend, and Lord. He bore my sins in His own body on the tree and when I accepted Him as Savior He forgave my sins, made me a new creature in Him, to live a new life with Him and for Him. I have found Him a Friend to whom I can go when doubts or problems arise: I dare not live a moment without Him. He has become my Lord: His purpose and path have become mine. He satisfies every longing of my soul. (Gunnar Lund, Yale University.)

As a student of medicine and therefore of practical science, I have been convinced of the reality of God and the infallibility of the Bible as the Word of God. This Book being the only authority on a most important subject—that of God and man—speaks with the utmost consistency and finality and power. It has demonstrated to me that life is infinitely more than a blind, hollow, materialistic existence. Through its unique message I have found the profound happiness of knowing Jesus Christ as my Savior and Master. It is not vague sentimentalism to say that He is as personally real to me as my own family. (Kenneth M. Scott, Pennsylvania.)

To me Christ is a miracle whereby I know I can be purged of all moral weakness and wickedness, and behold, as it were, a great light streaming down to me from heaven, like a Jacob's ladder, giving me a glimpse of a glorious reward beyond, attainable for me if I put on the armor of the Holy Spirit, and in His strength endure every temptation, unhappiness, and disappointment that the future may bring. Christ is the dynamic which gives my life all its purpose and meaning, the key which opens up to me the love and guidance of God the Father. I have founded my house of life upon Him, and I know it will never be shaken. (Gleason L. Archer, Harvard University.)

I believe that all men without exception are by nature sinners, alienated from God, and when thus utterly lost in sin the Son of God Himself came down to earth, and by shedding His blood upon the cross paid the infinite penalty of the guilty of the whole world. I believe he who thus receives Jesus Christ as his Savior is born again spiritually as definitely as his first birth, and, so born spiritually, has new privileges, appetites and affections; that he is one body with Christ the Head and will live with Him forever. I believe no man can save himself by good works, or by what is commonly known as a moral life. I believe Jesus Christ to be the Son of God, without human father, conceived by the Holy Ghost, born of the Virgin Mary. (Dr. Howard A. Kelly, internationally famous late professor of Obstetrics and Gynecology, Johns Hopkins University.)

Christ has saved me from sin—the devastating plague that smote soul and life. Christ has brought forgiveness and peace. "He daily loadeth me with benefits" as I yield mind and will captive to the power of His love. Christ has saved me from futilism and has given point and purpose to life. I find the telescopic and microscopic worlds declaring His purposes. History is no longer a series of accidents, but the unfolding of His purpose, and my part in the scheme of things is likewise purposeful. Christ the crown and climax of life! Christ the irreducible minimum! Christ the immeasurable maximum! I am complete in Christ. (James Forrester, Queen's University, Kingston, Ontario.)

A knowledge of Jesus Christ the Son of God, as one's personal Savior is the greatest hope and possession that one can have. Such a faith gives me something to live for and is the only hope for thousands of purposeless souls who have been blinded into indifference by Satan. The highest ideal in life is service; and while achieving some measure of success in running, I found it was only a corruptible crown and that material and earthly successes do not satisfy. Christ gave His life for me. I can have no higher ideal than that presented in Romans 12:1-2 and Colossians 3:12. Above all, I can be a happy Christian. (Elroy Robinson, Fresno State.)

Thus speak thousands of America's best youth today, in college and university, in business and the professions, in everyday, practical life, and where the miracle of life is to be proclaimed to others. And entire communities and groups are being transformed as our young people live the Christ they confess.

Should I add to their testimony the witness of countless numbers of our own young people as I have met them and heard their confession of faith, in schools and colleges, in conferences and conventions, in Bible camps and in the private confessional, in army camps and naval stations, or look at their letters coming from combat zones, there would be no end to the procession of witnesses. For thousands of our best youth today have learned by personal experience the hopelessness of a life lived separated from God. They see with their own eyes the chaotic despair that follows *their plans* who build without God. They have been present at great conferences where the name of Jesus Christ is exalted. They have seen the transforming and changing power of Christ's gospel in the lives of their friends as they have felt it in their own lives. They are rising up from the confessional and from the communion table changed men and women to take their place in society and in a world which so desperately needs the influence of their transformed lives. They have faced death on battlefields, on the seas, in the air, beneath the seas. And they are going out and living Jesus Christ in the world which now is, in a way which makes the communities which know them feel that a miracle of God has been performed before their eyes.

You who read these pages have, I am sure, begun to appreciate that you want to "live Christ now." You have heard Christ speak. You have listened to His pleading voice. You have heard His call. You have been warmed by His love. You have been given a vision of a redeemed and renewed world if His will is done among us. You have seen the boundary lines of the world pushed back —and now, I am sure, God is Himself reaching out His hands in benediction as you go out into the community He has set aside for you as your world—to live and work and serve and sacrifice and love, for Him and your fellow-men. There you can live your faith as He wants it lived! And there your daily confession can be:

This is my faith in Thee,
Tall Christ of Galilee:
Wherever I may be
    Thou art before,
Thou on the dizzying trail,
Thou in the shadowed vale,
Thou in the impassioned gale,
    Ever before.

Thou my soul's moving Guide
On with the unwearying stride,
Morning and eventide,
    Ever before;
On with unhastened breath,
Where my soul quivereth,
Into death, out of death,
    Ever before.

Thou my unwavering right,
Thou my unbroken light,
Thou my unsullied white,
    Ever before.
This is my faith in Thee,
Tall Christ of Galilee,
Wherever I may be,
    Thou art before.

(Robert Freeman)

And so we live Christ in the here and now—vitally, meaningfully, purposefully, completely, knowing that we belong to Him who died for us and believing that there is no greater glory that can come to us than to be worthy of the life in His name.

Today we will live for Christ and we will live Christ. We will live Christ now. For the present "now" is all the life we have to live. Yesterday is gone, with its sins and failures and disappointments and disasters. Yesterday already belongs to eternity.

To live "now" is all the living I can give my Savior and my world. Tomorrow belongs to God.

Today I am Christ's if I live for Him now. Tomorrow —tomorrow is God's. But Christ is God and God is Christ. Living Christ I am God's, for today, for tomorrow, for this world, for the world that is yet to be. For in eternity Christ is still God and I am His—forever!

Triumphant Living

It may seem strangely paradoxical that I want to add a word about victorious living. It seems to be utterly out of tune with realities as they are reported to us from every corner of the world. Not life, but death seems to abound, and horrible preparations for death as the forces of destruction are massed to destroy our present civilization. Not the abundant life do I read about in newspapers and magazines; but about an abundance of present circumstances combining to destroy life and mankind itself. All the world is preparing itself for a death struggle, which, when it comes, threatens to destroy the world as we know it now.

Still I should like to speak to you about life, and about God; for all my life I have wondered about life and about God. And I know now that you cannot truly live a life unless you live it with God. Without God life is not life at all. It is only existence. And you do not live when you only exist.

But more than this. I want to speak to you about victorious living. About triumphant living. And it is preeminently fitting that we should face such a theme at a time like this when all about us we behold evidences of the lifegiving power of God, where life is still being lived, though even now life is being denied to those who live in countries less favored than is ours.

Is there really such a thing as a victorious life?

I look about me today. There are so few evidences of victory. Indeed, the visible evidences of life are largely to the contrary. There is an abundance of evidence of futility. There is failure, defeat, despair, ignorance, unbelief, disobedience, frustration, sin, and death! And death stalks closer and closer, even if it is not violent death.

Too many there are who live futile and frustrated lives. There is in them no incentive, no light, no life, no ambition, no dynamic, no power, no victory, no overpowering desire to triumph, no hope. And their hopelessness is measured in the mediocrity of their plans, in their little living. A little work, a little gaiety, a few parties, blind-alley plans, a little happiness, a few joys, a few sorrows—and then oblivion and death. And they have not lived. Not at all! They do not even know what life is.

How many there are who live thus. I pick up my evening newspaper. Scandal here. Snuffed out lives there. An attorney leaps from the 86th floor of the Empire State building to sudden death. An actress commits suicide. A youth tried the fast life and awoke to defeat. A business man tried the dishonest way, only to live out his disgrace behind the bars of Sing Sing penitentiary. I am asked to speak at McNeil Island Federal Penitentiary and again at Alcatraz Federal Prison where Uncle Sam's number one prisoners are confined, the majority of them mere youths. At my side stand the armed guards, and beside and behind the prisoners, too. Ruined lives face me as I preach, ruined and full of hopeless despair. Futility of life seems enthroned. Victory belongs to the life of imagination and fiction.

But it doesn't. Every life can be the victorious life.

In us there are the seeds of defeat, to be sure, and these seeds are planted in the lives of all of us. For sin is there, outmoded as is the very idea; and sin always leads to defeat. But victory is there too; for faith can be brought into the heart. And faith is the victory that overcometh the world.

An old professor faced his classes at certain intervals with the challenging questions: "What am I? What ought I to be? How shall I get from what I am to what I ought to be?" I think he knew the answer, and I am sure he emphasized for his classes the eternal truth of the answer. For there is only one answer after all. I can become what I ought to be only through faith, faith in Him who is what we all should be, faith in Jesus Christ, who is life and light, perfection and salvation. For this faith has transforming power, and through it individuals and peoples are changed to live lives that count.

The challenge of the Scriptures is that "The just shall live by faith." The victorious life is the life of faith. Faith changes everything. Not only does it change things. It gives victory over the forces which otherwise and without it would pull us down. Faith gives victory over self and over all the forces of defeat and despair. Faith gives strength to change disobedience into obedience, sin into moral living, frustration into purpose, despair into hope, and defeat into power and ultimate victory. Through it, even faith is transformed into love. And love lives. Love takes the will and gives it the incentive and the eagerness to follow the directions of the will of God. Where God's will reigns, there can never be frustration, but only victory at last.

If we are to live victoriously, then we must live in the will of God. And it is His will, Scripture tells us, to believe in Him and in His Son, Jesus Christ, who has gained the victory of life for us.

Faith in Jesus Christ gives faith in self. Let us face that

fact. There are revolutionary changes which come with faith. We look upon ourselves, and strangely we find that self has changed. In a life transformed by faith, we discover new powers, new and unexpected capacities, the power to will and to do and to live and to die, victoriously. And more, much more! Faith in Christ gives faith in immortality. This life is not all. Nor is it the end. It is only a beginning. We can live here and gain power as we live, even though some God-haters now try to say this isn't true. But we live too in the hope of life to come, continuing life, transforming life, victorious life, triumphant life, eternal life. And who would not wish to live purposefully, when we know that we shall live eternally?

So we take this life which God has given us and live it according to His will, a life transformed by love for the Master. What happens?

In the first place, there is new direction to life. Life which seemed so purposeless is all of a sudden caught up in the great purposes of God. Life which seemed such a lonely experience is lived daily in company with God. Each moment it seems we stand before His presence. He walks with us and He talks with us and He tells us we are His own. The tasks we meet seem large, because they are to be done really for Him. There is purpose in all we do, because there are Kingdom purposes in our lives. There are accomplishments to be striven for, because each accomplishment seems a victory for His cause. There are sacrifices to be made gladly, because each sacrifice is in harmony with the great sacrifice He made for us when He gave His Son to save us.

And so life, each day of it, each moment, becomes full of purpose and rich in experience, because purpose and accomplishment seem joined in the life we live with Him. No more is there an empty morning, nor a meaningless night. There is the day between, and this day is a life, not to be lived for ourselves in day dreaming or in night carousing, but a life given by Him and to be lived for Him, who once lived and died for us.

The perfect life of Christ was a life of sacrifice lived through love. Sacrificial love makes weakness turn into strength, cowardice into courage, inferiority into power, disobedience into obedience, indifference into eagerness, unwillingness into willingness, selfishness into self-sacrifice, and defeat and frustration into victory.

Triumphant lives are described in the Book of Hebrews as lives of great faith and these lives are lived in every age and in every place where Jesus Christ has by His transforming power changed will and heart into the glorious experience of fellowship and discipleship with Him. Where these have been given preeminence through faith in the power of His name, there there is life and the transforming purpose of living as He wants His followers to live.

Such lives are being lived now, and neither fire nor famine, neither sword nor dungeon, neither the gallows nor horrible death can stop their testimony. The mission lands are producing these heroes by the thousands. And in other lands in most unexpected places, in most unexpected personalities, I see this new power at work. It is even now taking hold of great men of science like Dr. Arthur Compton, physicist and Nobel prize winner, and making him burst forth in his paean of gladness as he tells about his faith in immortality. It is taking hold of great leaders of the world like General and Madame Chiang Kai-shek, making this president of a war-torn republic broadcast to the world his Easter message: "Why I believe in Jesus Christ." Or of that great hero of the World War, Martin Niemoller, making him stand out today before all the world as a twentieth century hero of our Christian faith. Or to thousands and tens of thousands of our young people making them stand out today as the great hope for a world in chaos because of their faith in Jesus Christ.

Love for Jesus Christ brings with it an all-inclusive transformation. Love drives out hatred as it casts out fear. Love brings about a reconciliation between God and man as it brings about relations of sincere fellowship with fellowmen. Love gives dynamic to action, desire for service, eagerness to sacrifice, joy untold in living.

Love is like God; for God is love. All else shall pass away but love lasts forever. It is the one virtue which has eternal significance. It gives life its victorious tone here as it gives it its triumphant significance in heaven. Eternal life is eternal love. Eternal life is perfect love to Christ. So life *must* be eternally triumphant, if it is wrapped up in and motivated by the love of Jesus Christ.

The triumphant, victorious life is the life in Christ, the Christian life. And those have it who have seen and felt His saving love. If you have met Jesus Christ, if His love has warmed your heart and saved your soul, then you have this life now. You are living it. You are living victoriously, you are living a transformed life, no matter if the world has never seen the victory or heard of the conquest Christ made in you.

And if you want to live this life more fully, if you want to live it victoriously, if you want to grow in it as you grow in grace and holiness, if you want to live courageously and heroically, then there is a way to achieve. You can reach the goal. Everyone can. For into our midst there has come an unseen power, who is the miracle of the Word of God. It is the Spirit of God whom Christ promised as His special gift of grace before He left this earth. He is truth and He is life. He creates life. He gives us faith as He gives us the power to live. To live triumphantly is to live in the power He gives.

This is the power the world needs today, needs desperately. All of us need it to overcome the inroads of sin.

Those who have it do not live for themselves. They live for others. And those who have learned to live for others, for Christ, for God, they have gained the victory which shall overcome the world.

Those who do not possess this power can get it. It is to be had for the asking. Go to God's Word with a seeking and a believing heart. God's Spirit will reveal it to you there and give it to you at last. For it comes as a free gift to all those who believe in Jesus Christ as the Son of God.

It is amazing, when you hear the story, the transforming change which takes place when the life in Jesus Christ is permitted to reveal itself in all its saving power. Defeated lives are changed into victorious lives, and the changing of an individual life can often have results which influence the life of a nation and a generation.

Some time ago there came to my desk a letter from a chaplain in the Italian theatre of war which to me seems to breathe that spirit of victorious faith which has the promise of overcoming the world.

I think I shall let his letter stand as it came and let it carry its own message. Its every word breathes a message of victory, of triumphant Christian faith even where a world is crumbling into decay. I wonder, too, if it will not explain to some of us some of the hidden purposes of God in permitting the present course of the war to reach its own mysterious goal.

Some months ago I received a communication from you which stated that a great deal depended upon Protestant Army Chaplains in reference to the way in which the evangelical Christian faith would be spread in the future in countries now occupied by the U. S. armed forces. The French Catholic faith came in conjointly with the French occupation of North Africa forty years ago. Would the entrance of American troops and Protestant Chaplains make the evangelical Protestant faith also a reality to some people in Africa, Sicily, and Italy? The tenor and text of your message was that Chaplains were missionaries representing their Lord in a strange land.

It seems strange that the Holy Spirit should have given you this message just a little before I was to experience it and see it.

Two months ago I was flown into Sicily to serve as Base Chaplain to all U. S. Army Air Corps Troops stationed in Sicily. Our Group was the Base outfit and everything in the island was subject to us in point of administration.

A dr. —— [name withheld for obvious reasons], a graduate of three European Universities, a descendant of the Royal Bourbon family of North Italy in the employ of AMGOT (Allied Government Military Officials) , and a brilliant linguist in six languages, sought me out almost with the first step that I took off from the transport plane onto Sicily's soil. He took me by the hand and said: "If you are a Protestant Chaplain, God has sent you to me. I have been waiting for you for many years. You must tell me what you know concerning the Bible." His father had had him baptized Catholic, and his mother had been a Protestant and had died at an early age, a descendant of the Waldensians, Piedmont, North Italy. This son had remembered his mother telling him how different the Protestants' approach to God was from that taught in his church. He took me into his home and introduced me to the most select circles of the city. I had the great joy of instructing him privately, at his request, in Luther's Small Catechism, and as its vistas of truth opened out before him each day, he seemed to learn more and more each day. He clung to me almost as a little child and finally said: "You Protestants have a heart religion. It is deep and a terrible thing to be a Protestant and to understand God's angered Law rather than an outward observance of rites, and to understand that Christ's atonement makes up for the broken law. When you Protestants pray you pray directly from the heart to your God and do not recite nor read your prayers as we do." Every time after instruction I had him pray on bended knee with me, and always it seemed that it was the prayers that helped him the most. He said that after his instruction a strange hush would be over him for the remainder of the day. He is now ready to be confirmed. [He has since been confirmed and given membership in the Waldensian Church as there is no Lutheran Church in Sicily.]

This is one of the most outstanding cases of conversions that I have ever seen on foreign soil, and I believe that it will be a lasting and substantial one, and coming from a man of wealth and influence and standing and position in the community, I believe that it will count in the future history of the city in which the man resides here in Sicily. The man is a frank, openhearted, great, and generous soul, and says that his son will be baptized Protestant and that he believes that his wife will follow in his footsteps also.

I have given him abundant Protestant literature and among it also your Service Prayer Book. I could use 100 more copies of your Prayer Book. I will never forget how bomber pilots, gunners, and mechanics took your Service Prayer Book at the end of our church services out on Cape Bon. They walked off silently reading it, and the next day was their turn to make their mission out over the enemy and some of those men never came back. All Protestant Chaplains ask for your Service Prayer Book. I notice it as a part of their bookshelves, available in large station hospitals, and packed and re-packed in our Army's constant moving. Many of the men carry it with them all of the time, so I do want you to know that it has been used, and used constantly. At Souk El Arba, Tunisia, many British Chaplains came in and begged me for ten copies of it saying that it would only go out where men were eithei Christians or where they were prospective Christians. When I was at Souk El Arba I was at the heart of General Anderson's First Army H. Q. (British) and the British would have been glad to take all of my Prayer Books in one day. But I had to put a stop to it, and direct them back to their own Chaplains. I am deeply happy that that little prayer book has been given out to the world, and at that by the Lutheran Church.

So lives the victorious, the triumphant life, in constant dependence upon and in continual faith in Jesus Christ, our Lord.

Power for This Day

Long, long time ago—so long that too many men have all but forgotten that He ever lived—a young man walked one day the dusty roads of Galilee up to the city of God. He was met with a frenzy of enthusiasm by a people who hailed Him as king, even though He came riding on the foal of an ass. They wanted to place Him on the throne of David. They did not understand when He said: "My kingdom is not of this world." But when they realized that He would not and could not acquiesce to their demands, they as quickly repudiated Him, cast Him aside, and rejected Him.

A few days later I see Him again, a long night it was, suffering the agony of hell because He realized the people knew not the day of their visitation. They had denied and renounced Him. They had forgotten and had lost God.

The next day, very early it was, He was walking another road, a narrow, crooked lane it was, called to this day the Via Dolorosa, the way of sorrows. Stumbling were His feet, heavy His load beneath the awful burden of the cross they had laid across His shoulders—called the sorrows of all the world.

On and on He stumbled, cursed by the jibes and jeers of a mob bent now upon His horrible death. At last He can carry His load no farther. Into the dust and grime of a dirty street He falls with the cross crushing Him down until, seeing His suffering, the women cry out against it all. But He, noticing their tears, speaks to them: "Weep not for me! But weep rather for yourselves and for your children" and your children's children. And sometimes when I try to visualize it all, it seems to me He must have foreseen this year of our Lord, when beneath the awful anguish of war, womanhood and motherhood everywhere, mothers, wives, sweethearts, sisters, in all lands, are crying out against the horror which is separating and robbing them of all that is dear in life.

Everywhere I go today as I travel from city to city, I see the agony of separation from loved ones in stations and at trains. Till at last I can look at the anguish of crushed lives no longer and my heart cries out: "O Lord, how long, how long!"

All this grief He saw and He bore that day as He lifted again His cross to stumble up the steep road that led to the hill "outside a city wall," the hill called Calvary.

Calvary! But in that day they called it in their language Golgotha, the place of skulls. The place of skulls, the place of dead men's bones! Dead men's hill! And up there they fixed Jesus Christ, Son of God and Son of man, with cruel hands to His cross and flung it and Him up against the skies which His own hands with divine power one time themselves had fashioned.

He died there that day. He died! And they thought Him well dead, even though strangely He died before the appointed time.

But now suddenly the consciences of His executioners became furiously active. They remembered His cryptic words about a resurrection. Hurriedly they took His dead body down from the cross, called the cross now of the sins of the world. With unsympathetic hands they laid Him out in an open tomb. And then to be sure He would trouble them no more, they ran down to Pontius Pilate to get his permission to seal the tomb against the possibility of ghouls who might want to rob His body and say that He was risen from the dead.

Soldiers were dispatched with ribbon and wax to fix the face of a weak Hitler in Rome to the face of the great stone which closed the tomb. And now all the world was to know that this man was dead.

The three days of Scripture were at an end which was to mark His stay among the dead. Then early in the morning of the third day, of His own will and power, this young man rose to place His feet again upon the earth His hands had made. And immediately there was a quaking and a shaking of the earth, terrible as at Judgment Day. And Jesus Christ walked forth in power and great majesty and glory, King of kings now, Lord of lords, God of gods, with a glory which all could see, even the guard at the grave: "Surely this man was the Son of God."

Perhaps it is not so strange that in the chapters of the gospels which follow the event of the resurrection, He is ever after called only the *Lord* Jesus Christ!

And then I see this young man another day walking again the roads of Galilee, although invisible now because of the strange power which was His, to meet by prearrangement His disciples and apostles on one of the lofty hills of the Galilean province. Suddenly and mysteriously He was seen sitting in their midst. How He came and from where they did not know. They only realized it was He, when they heard Him speak.

Gently He spoke as a friend speaks to friends he knows and trusts. About the Kingdom of God He spoke. He explained to them things they should know, things which must help them in the hard days ahead.

He spoke of the future, about the world spread of the gospel message. And sometimes I wonder again if that day His mind's eye did not foresee all of the tragedies of this year of our Lord when catastrophic events should transpire, and chaos such as will precede the Day of Judgment come to pass.

They were listening intently, careful lest they miss a word, looking down and thinking in the fashion of Rodin's famous masterpiece, "The Thinker."

Then gradually they became conscious of a great change in His voice—no longer the pleading voice of friend and teacher and savior. Now suddenly clothed with infinite power and majesty they heard Him speak in language they had never heard before, and were never to hear again, until He speaks at last on Judgment Day:

"All authority has been given to me in heaven and in earth. Go ye therefore, and make disciples of all the nations, baptizing them into the name of the Father, and of the Son, and of the Holy Spirit: teaching them to observe all things whatsoever I have commanded you: and lo, I am with you alway, even unto the end of the world." Unto the end of the world—the end of the world! And then there was no more. Only a great silence as before the dawn of a new day.

They looked up in startled surprise. But He was gone! They saw Him nowhere. Up and up their eyes lifted as we lift our eyes to see great planes pass through the clouds. There finally they saw Him. Just a glimpse, as He was passing back of a shining cloud. But the Christ they saw was the Christ of the outstretched arms, lifted in a last benediction upon a world which knew not the day of its visitation.

How alike we are to the world of that day and akin to those who knew Him not, we of this generation!

Like that day, tragedy has come upon the earth like the tragedy of doomsday. And like that generation, ours faces doomsday in a spirit of thoughtless indifference or bold rebellion. We, like them, have rejected and lost God. We, like them, have renounced and repudiated the Christ. We, like them, have ridiculed the miraculous power of God, and, laughing it off, we have come under their condemnation.

We have even taught our children disrespect for all that is holy. Having lost God ourselves, we have taught our children the insecure ways of the sophisticate. In schools and colleges we have laughed at the miraculous and the supernatural. We have insisted on walking our own ways and our children to walk theirs, till of a sudden we face a generation which in the terminology of the day was to be known as "the lost generation."

There was no power in us or in them. Just the easy tempo of the spiritually illiterate as we danced and drank our way into destruction.

But then came tragedy, swift and merciless, as the destruction which waits at noonday. Because we had lost God, we had no eyes to see nor ears to hear His warning which always comes before doomsday: "Counted, weighed, found wanting." And no sudden tears, no change of dress into the dress of sackcloth and ashes, no cry to high heaven could stay the destruction which was to engulf us and the world. In the day of our greatest pride and our easiest boast, we saw our children, sons and daughters, an entire generation of our youth, this lost generation, going out to face death because we had failed and, failing, had lost God.

All the while Jesus Christ was there as in the days of Gethsemane and Calvary and Easter and the Ascension and Pentecost, with guidance and comfort, compassion and mercy, power and majesty and glory enough to cover us all, if we could only lift up our eyes as did His disciples on the Mount of Transfiguration and Ascension, and see Him as He really is.

How strange it is that it is this lost generation, gone now to the ends of the earth, facing death everywhere in a thousand cruel ways—how strange it is that it is this generation, the lost generation, who should again discover the miraculous in God and the saving power and glory in the gospel which tells them about His Savior Son!

How strange it is, too, that it should be in this day of tragedy and chaos and catastrophe, when our enemies boast only of the power of might and the security and invincibility of fortifications and arms, that this nation which is ours should discover the need for another Power besides the power of military might.

For we have suddenly come to realize that armor and force can mean destruction of all ideals unless they are possessed by men who above all fear the might of the living God. Strange, is it not, that in this day of testing we should discover the power of faith in God. Strange, is it not, that we today should rob ten thousand pulpits of their pastors to send them with ten million men who must fight and die, to go with them; teach them the ways of God; preach to them the love and mercy of God; show them a Savior always ready to save. And then themselves go with them to live with these young heroes of ours; help them prevail in a day of great temptation; reveal to them God as He verily is; and on the field of battle go with them, bind up their wounds, and for the dying show them the way through the valley of the shadow of death to the place where the risen and ascended Savior Lord stands ready to receive those that are His into the shining glory of Kingdom Come.

Everywhere they and their men are seeing their Lord as He is. Everywhere He is revealing Himself in all His majestic glory and His saving love. Countless souls have seen and believed.

There is power in this Christ for this day as there has been in the past and as there shall be forevermore for all those who, discovering Him now, have found Him to be all He ever claimed to be.

A few months ago I had a letter from a chaplain who since then has gone with his men through the Tunisian campaign and the catastrophe of the Kasserine pass, through the Sicilian and now the Italian campaign. He wrote about a service he conducted for his men the night before their first battle in Tunisia.

I made preparations for this service, all the time thinking that only a few would come. You see, there are other things to attend to the night before battle, a thousand duties which must not be neglected if our plans shall meet with success.

But there they were that night, crowding every available inch of space, officers and men.

Our services must necessarily be very simple in battle areas. There are no organs or pianos or orchestras or bands to make the services festive here.

So all I could do was to reach out for some old hymn which I could hope might be familiar. Shall we sing: "What a friend we have in Jesus"? I said.

I have never heard singing like that. All at once they were all singing the four parts of the music. From their hearts they sang as though they were standing before the throne of God.

That is the difference between their singing and ours. We, when and if we go to church, sing with a listlessness which must agonize the heart of God, as if we had an eternity of living ahead of us. They sing out there as if they know that eternity is just ahead, and that the next moment they may be facing God. He continues:

And then I preached as simply as I could on that great Old Testament gospel Psalm: "The Lord is my Shepherd, I shall not want. . . . Yea, though I walk through the valley of the shadow of death I shall fear no evil, for thou art with me, thy rod and thy staff they comfort me. . . . And I shall dwell in the house of the Lord forever."

How they listened! How earnestly attentive they were!

Then I handed out your stationery, and quietly each lad sought out a place where he could write a last note home to mother.

The censorship officer came in later to pick up the letters, as he must.

Late that night this officer came to my tent. "Chaplain," he said, "you have never known me as a religious man. You have never seen me at any of your services. I was one of those smart fellows who thought he could nicely and easily get along without God. I never cared for God or thought I owed Him anything, if He exists.

"But I must have missed something, something very real. I have been reading the letters of these men written home to their mothers tonight. Do you know, chaplain, there wasn't a lad present at your service but what he told his mother the comfort and the courage that came to him listening to your sermon with its promise of a shepherd Lord who would go all the way into battle and death on the morrow. Chaplain, I must have missed something. You will see me at services hereafter. I want to know the Lord who has promised power sufficient even for the tragedy which faces us now."

It was like the experience of the young service man who, upset and utterly at sea in his thinking about the why of life, chanced into a certain Center, where, thank God, a young Christian woman was destined by Him who knows all to meet him in his hour of need.

I was lonely as can be and frightened about sailing out again. I wanted to talk to someone badly. This girl smiled and said hello to me. She said for me to sit down, and we began talking about the future. I felt that there probably was no future for me. If only a fellow could be sure, I remarked, that something would come through worth dying for, it wouldn't be so bad.

The girl said the queerest thing. She smiled and said, "That's easy! Christ is coming through and He's worth dying for."

I looked at her, and she kept talking as if He were right

there and a good pal of hers. I sort of expected to see Him come right through the door; it was so real.

I was there only a few minutes. I do not know why, but her talking did something to me. I am not lonely any more, and I am not afraid. It was just as she said to me, "You ought to get to know each other, since *He will be going your way.*"

I am nineteen, and I never knew there was a God like that who would go along with a fellow. It doesn't matter so much now if my ship goes down and I go down with it as long as there is One whom no sub can sink and who won't ever change from what's right, even if this war goes on forever!

"Jesus Christ the same yesterday, and today, and forever!" (Hebrews 13:8.)

I was speaking at Carnegie Hall in Pittsburgh one evening and I told the following story which had just come to me and was later verified by ranking officers whose families I have known for many years. How startled I was when a note was passed up to me from the audience that night saying that the parents of Private Paul Beiswenger, one of the central figures in the story, were in the audience and wanted to speak to me. They verified the story as I knew it then. It was later I heard the sequel.

This is the story I told, cabled partly to *Time Magazine,* and verified by one of our senior Marine Corps Chaplains who wrote me that it was the Service Prayer Book that I had compiled which was the prayerbook used those long days between that dramatic crash landing and the final rescue of the wounded veterans of Guadalcanal and the transport plane's crew:

It was four days since the big Douglas transport, carrying seventeen sick and wounded soldiers, sailors, and marines, besides its own crew, from Henderson Field, Guadalcanal, which was under heavy attack, had been forced to make a crash landing on a coral reef somewhere in the Pacific.

The landing itself was a miracle of God. The pilot, son of a Methodist minister, himself a Christian, had seen from the air the submerged coral reef on which by divine assistance he placed his big ship with a perfect landing maneuver. The crash landing was made necessary because in its escape from the island both radio and radio compass had been knocked out, the transport plane losing its way during the ensuing night, and by dawn consequently found itself without gas to continue. The plane settled on the coral reef only partly submerged. So the crew rigged up a spider web of parachute ropes under the ceiling of the plane and here most of the seriously wounded were suspended for eleven days.

During those endless days some were stricken with malaria and others suffered extreme pain from their untended wounds. Food supplies were running low and drinking water was only obtained by catching rainwater in their helmets.

Sunday was the fifth day and hope of rescue had practically vanished. Suddenly "Buck" Torrente, a nineteen year old from Manhattan, observed out loud, "What do you know! Here it's Sunday. If I were home today I'd be walking home from St. Veronica's Church about now!"

In the silence of the cabin, Private Paul Beiswenger from Pittsburgh hunted through his pack and found his Service Prayer Book. He handed it to Ensign M. E. Herbst and said: "Will you conduct the service, sir?"

Ensign Herbst opened the book. In a high-pitched voice he read the prayers as they came. The men in the cabin bowed their heads. For thirty minutes Herbst read, until he came to a prayer for sailors in storms at sea: "Oh most powerful and glorious Lord God, at whose command the winds blow and lift up the waves of the sea, and who stillest the rage thereof . . . we cry unto Thee for help. . . ."

When he said "Amen," "Buck" Torrente began the hymn "O Thou and the Lord." Some sang, some hummed. Marine Sergeant Steve Kupiec remembered the words of "O Lord, I am not worthy." Herbst closed the prayer book and announced: "That will be all till next Sunday."

But now comes the unpublished sequel which was told me in a letter some time after these men were rescued by a destroyer and three PBY boats.

Up in the pilot's cabin during all these days sat a wounded Marine Corps Major and a Lieutenant Colonel. The major is a member of our church and a professing Christian who has since this experience often publicly urged on his hearers the real meaning and the urgency of effective prayer. The lieutenant colonel was an unbeliever.

The major spent much of the eleven days reading his New Testament which he always carried with him. Finally, one day the colonel crossly said: "Let me see that book you are so constantly reading."

From that moment it was the colonel who became the avid reader. When finally rescue came, it was he who offered the public prayer of thanksgiving to God for saving him and these shipwrecked men, and it was he who asked them all to join with him in publicly praying together the Lord's Prayer in praise of Him who had the power to save.

No, we aren't talking about fox-hole religion now, nor the fetish so many are making of prayer and the thing some call religion. It is one thing to be religious and something quite different to be Christian. It is one thing to know the fear of God in the face of death, something else to know the comfort and courage which come with Christian faith.

But how many evidences there are now of the power and efficacy of Christian faith!

A young chaplain was to go into battle with his men. In battle the chaplain divests himself of all evidences of rank. Only the silver crosses on his lapels show his men that at their side is a man of God.

This chaplain was afraid that in the smoke and dust and confusion of battle his men might fail to recognize his crosses. So just before the zero hour he contrived with the help of some white paint and a brush to paint a bold white cross on the front of his steel helmet. And so he went into battle in the front line wave as a chaplain will.

The thing he expected, happened. A young lad fell mortally wounded at his side. The chaplain, kneeling down, saw the lad had only a few moments to live. He told him the age old story of a Savior's love, how his Lord would go with him through the valley of death and lead him home to God.

The lad's unblinking eyes seemed fixed on the chaplain's. But suddenly the chaplain knew the lad was not looking into the chaplain's eyes at all. Then he remembered. It was at the cross on his helmet the dying lad was staring. And he died there that day—with his eyes fixed on the cross.

I would give all the world to have been that chaplain. And I would give all the world to be permitted to die like that, with my eyes fixed on the cross, the cross on which my Savior died.

Power for this day? How the evidences multiply, and how many they are who experience it! In another letter a friend of mine wrote:

I was a Base Chaplain. I served Army and Navy air units. I served transient fighter and bomber units and units shuttling in from Britain. Air Transport units from all the way to Liberia, Iran, and Bombay stopped for a breathing spell at our station. One night one of the finest, most clean-cut young air pilots that I have ever seen, with large intelligent looking brown eyes, sat across the table from me at officers' mess as a transient Air Transport pilot, flying Central Africa.

On seeing the cross insignia on my collar, he immediately asked, "Chaplain, when do you have church services?" I said: "I have a midweek Bible study and Prayer service tonight." "Fine," he replied, "I will be there."

He was there and he showed that he had an intimate knowledge and love of the Bible by the part that he took in the discussion, and in the prayer period that followed he offered a beautiful Christian prayer. Some splendid free prayers were offered that night by a large number of men. Afterward the Transient pilot asked for Holy Communion. As I brought out my beautiful Lutheran Communion Set provided by the National Lutheran Council, he expressed astonishment and pleasure. "I am a Lutheran from Trinity Lutheran Church of Moline, Illinois," he said, "but I never expected to find Mother Church meeting me like this in darkest Africa." Very early next morning he was off for Algiers.

Six months later I was holding a vespers for Bomb Group pilots who were as tense as high strung athletes with the task of repeated bombing missions over Italy staring them in the face.

Who should come forward after the crowded service but my friend of six months ago. "Chaplain, I am glad to see you again," he said as he grasped my hand. "Do come and hold a midweek service for us."

I came to hold the service, but he was not there. His plane was one of three to be shot down over the target. I lost a friend, yesterday. I lost a friend!

The power for today is there in abundant measure for all who will have it. And Jesus Christ is abundantly able to save to the uttermost even this generation whom yesterday men called "the lost generation."

Christ is still the power of God unto salvation to all who will believe. He is the light of the world, shining brightly in the encircling gloom so all who will may see Him. "The light shineth in darkness but as of yore so many comprehend it not. Jesus is the true Light, which lighteth every man that cometh into the world. He was in the world, and the world was made by him, and the world knew him not. He came unto his own, and his own received him not. But as many as received him, to them gave he power to become the sons of God, even to them that believe on his name; which were born, not of blood, nor of the will of the flesh, nor of the will of man, but of God" (John 1:5; 9-13).

"Give me a light," said a dying lad on the battlefield to his chaplain. The chaplain, misunderstanding him, began fumbling in his pocket for cigarette and matches. "No, not that kind of light, chaplain. There is only one kind of light which will help me now. Give me the light that will lighten the way through the dark shadows of the valley of death and show me the way home to God. That is where I am going now."

And Jesus Christ is still the same, yesterday, today, and forever. He still has the power we need for this day, to save to the very uttermost.

Trumpets Sounding
from the Other Side

("In Memoriam" to Heroes of World War II)

CHAPTER XIV

It was several years ago. We were visiting Rothenburg in the heart of Germany, one of the quaintest of the medieval cities in the yesterday that was. Walled and turreted, with deep moats and lofty towers, we saw it that day as Luther saw it in the long ago and as Gustav Adolph saw it a hundred years later. We had stood on the high walls to look out upon a distant plain, the battlefield where was fought one of the decisive battles of the Thirty Years War and of all history.

At noon we assembled in the town square beneath the central lofty tower of the town. Suddenly from the belfry of the tower, high up towards heaven, came a sound we were to remember long—the brass chorus of trumpeters sounding the memorial dirge for warriors long since dead, and the call to arms for a Germany once again on the march toward hoped-for world domination.

How strange was that trumpet music, and how weirdly impressive and challenging! Like the call to arms from another generation!

We stood one day on the battlefield of Stiklestad, Norway, with 30,000 others who had come from the ends of the earth to celebrate the 900th memorial of a victory gained by a king and his men, consecrated to the onward march of the Kingdom of God. A nation was on its feet to do honor to the memory of this sainted king. A king of heroic stature and historic name challenged anew his people to be faithful to the God of their fathers. And a bishop of God picked up the trumpet of God that day and sounded the call of the armies of God to march forward for country and God, with a note which the people of his land were never again to forget.

How unbelievable that only ten years later a country which had celebrated that memorial day with festivity and song should lie prostrate beneath the heel of a cruel conqueror; that a king should pine away in exile; and that this bishop of God should from the anguish of an enemy concentration camp take up the trumpet of God and sound again to his people a call to arms which has been heard now around the world!

Memorial days can be days of God, and each memorial day may be a day of visitation from God, if the trumpets which sound are trumpets of God.

Today we remember God and remember those whose sacrifices and privations, whose sufferings and anguish, whose toil and hopes, whose blood and death have made sacred the pages of our history and whose dedication to a great task has made of our land a land of destiny and of our church a church which has brought untold blessing to the world.

You cannot stand today on the battlefields of this land where patriots met the challenge of the duties of their day without hearing again the echo of trumpets of God, calling us all to remember and forget not Him whose we are and whom we serve.

Ride the Pike Road of Paul Revere, stand at the little

bridge at Lexington, rise up with Lincoln by the countless graves of martyred hosts at Gettysburg and face with
him the tortured dead the day he spoke his immortal
words. Look long at the cyclorama of the battle of Atlan-
ta, or stand silently before the little tower of the Alamo,
and if you cannot hear again the trumpets of God sounding the requiem over honored dead, or hear in the chambers of your souls the resounding echoes of trumpets
sounding from the other side, you are dead to the implications of those sacred moments of history, and spiritually dead to the great call which today comes challenging
us from the other side, where patriots and prophets,
great heroes of the world and ageless heroes of God, are
ever anew crying out to us not to miss the intentions of
this new day of visitation that has come from God.

And even though the battlefields may have new and
difficult names today, names we never identified before;
even though our sons must fight and die at Guadalcanal,
and Tarawa, at Kasserine Pass, and at Cassino, the
trumpet call is the same and the sound of trumpets coming from the other side carries the same solemn notes,
sounds which spell hardship and toil, blood and sweat
and tears, separation and dedication, memories and
memorials, that these dead shall not have died in vain,
and that we who live shall not fail to measure up to the
blessings their consecrated lives have brought us.

A few years ago we were still a peaceful nation with
little, too little, to disturb the indifference of our careless ways. Two years ago there were already empty pews
at our worship services, with men of the church and
their pastors gone out to prepare for war or gone to far
off places where the din of awful battle was already
sounding in jungles and deserts and volcanic isles.

Two years ago sons of our church and their pastors
had already been tested in the awful caldron of mortal
combat.

Now their empty places cry out to us from empty homes and vacant pulpits and pews.

Two years ago a mother in one of our parsonages, concerned about the call to duty of her chaplain son, asked what could be done to bring to his worship services those who with him were being trained to face death. How hollow our answer sounded the day of her anguished question when I replied: "Your chaplain son will not have to worry about a hearing if he sounds to his men the trumpet of God, and brings them the message of the everlasting gospel."

Today her chaplain son has returned with his men from battle in the far off battle hells of Guadalcanal and Tarawa, with double presidential citations for extreme heroism beyond the call of duty. But the anxiety of yesterday has proved the eternal truth of the promise given. For the night before Tarawa 450 men of his battalion crowded the space set aside on board for a final worship and prayer service. 230 knelt at the altar of God to beg for and receive the assurance of forgiveness and grace, and others entered the Kingdom through Christian baptism performed in the presence of a congregation which had seen God.

At the close of the service the battlewagons spoke with a voice of sudden fury and with a sound like the voice of doom, and destruction reigned such as has not been seen on the earth. And chaplain and men went into the raging surf to face almost certain death in a frontal attack on 5,000 enemies still fighting to the death. Everywhere there was death and destruction. Casualties such as have not been recorded heretofore in the history of the Marine Corps.

But even in the face of murderous machine-gun fire, and blasting bombs, God was there, and His servant was there, miraculously protected. The wounded and the dying were ministered to in the face of impending death, the dead were identified and given Christian burial. And the next day a memorial service for the fallen was held on the stricken but captured island, where God was so close that none of the survivors will ever forget again the sound of the trumpet call in memory of their fallen comrades.

Nor will the chaplain be able to erase from his memory the souls which sought him that last night at the worship service, at the communion rail, and at the baptismal font, souls who now are standing in the presence of God listening to the sound of angel trumpets and angel choirs, in that land where suffering and death shall be no more.

Two years ago one of our young chaplains, able to get into the army only by sheer insistence of eagerness to serve, had just left our midst for arduous duties in training camps here. Now he is a veteran of the African campaign and of the Sicilian campaign and of the Italian campaign. He wears the silver star which tells a story of heroic ministry to his men in the face of death. More than a year he and his men have heard the nerve-shattering noise of bursting shells and exploding bombs, till he must cry out: "I wonder how much longer my men can stand all this."

But the other day he wrote to me again from the awful hell of battle in Italy. He wrote on a scrap of torn paper a note which bore all the stains of agony in battle. Enclosed in the letter was a poem found on the dead body of somebody's son.

You will perhaps be shocked at the crudeness of the dead man's theology, but you can never forget his anguished cry for the heart of God. I wonder if he heard that day he fell in battle "all the trumpets of God" the pilgrim in Pilgrim's Progress heard, "sounding for him on the other side."

Look, God, I have never spoken to You,
   But now I want to say "How do you do."
You see, God, they told me You didn't exist,
And like a fool I believed all this.

Last night, from a shell hole I saw Your sky.
   I figured right then they had told me a lie.
Had I taken time to see things You made,
I'd have known they weren't calling a spade a spade.

I wonder, God, if You'd shake my hand,
   Somehow I feel that You will understand.
Funny I had to come to this hellish place
Before I had time to see Your face.

Well, I guess there isn't much more to say,
   But I'm sure glad, God, I met You today.
I guess the zero hour will soon be here,
But I'm not afraid since I know You're here.

The signal! Well, God, I'll have to go,
   I like You lots, this I want You to know.
Look now, this will be a horrible fight,
Who knows, I may come to Your house tonight.

Though I wasn't friendly to You before
   I wonder, God, if You'd wait at Your door.
Look, I'm crying! Me! Shedding tears!
I wish I had known You these many years.

Well, I have to go now, God, goodbye!
   Strange, since I met You, I'm not afraid to die.
            ("Facing the Zero Hour." Author not given)

But memorial days are memorial days, indeed, only if
the trumpets of God sounding in requiem over our heroic
dead and in recognition for all those others who, living,
performed so valiantly for us, sound at the same time
to us who still live the call to eager duty, to sacred

responsibility, and to passionate zeal for a life worthy
of a day of testing and a day of destiny such as we face
together today. Unless the trumpets of God are sounded
so loudly and so clearly now that all of us are aroused
to a life of consecrated toil for a world which has lost
God and to a life of dedicated service in the Kingdom
of God which only has power to give new life, we will
have failed of the challenge of this hour. We will never
prove worthy of this day if we rise not now to perform
the tasks of consecrated servants of God.

It will not do in this day of destiny to revel too long
or too much in memories of a past which to many of us
may seem to have included days of shining glory and
of great deeds, magnified by the heroic stature of fore-
bears whose names may be inscribed on the pages of history as giants in the earth and great men of God.

This is no day for small men to pick up tin whistles
to sound the squeaky shibboleths of a dead past.

Our fathers, could they but see our world now in all
its tragedy and travail, would rejoice with exceeding
great joy, if, remembering that it was the Kingdom of
God they tried to serve, we now in their spirit arise, gird
ourselves to battle, and with the living Christ to guide,
march forth to battle for right and truth and justice and
freedom and salvation in a world which so desperately
needs the inspiring and consecrated leadership of real
men of God.

Think you that our problems are not great; that our
difficulties are not mountainous; that there is not a call
to high duty and noble accomplishment? Think you that
we can fritter away our time on irritating misunderstand-
ings, small tasks, and little deeds in this day when a
world is crying out for the living God, and in a day
when a suffering and starving and dying humanity is
begging for the lifegiving bread of life?

Up, up, ye men of God! The trumpets are sounding

everywhere. There are tasks to assume which can no longer wait. There are deeds to be done which must be done now. Eternity waits, but it waits not long for those who should know the way.

Or must it be said of us in this day of testing what a prophet of doom said to his church the other day as he reminded them of their signal failures:

> Like a halting caravan
> Moves the Church of Christ;
> We are feebly faltering
> Toward our timid tryst.
> We are all divided,
> Many bodies we,
> Kept apart by doctrine
> And lack of charity.
> Careful, Christian pilgrims!
> Walk in doubt and fear,
> With the Cross of Jesus
> Bringing up the rear.
> (Wm. H. Hudnut Jr., in *The Christian Century*)

No, this is not the day for cynics, nor doubters, nor the fearful, nor for small men whistling in the dark. This is the day of battle for men of great stature, deep and abiding faith, never-wavering convictions, calm with the calmness of eternity, serene with their faith fixed on God, "with the cross of Jesus going on before." This is not a day of timidity and pessimism and defeatism and despair. This is a day when a world is experiencing the agonies of a new birth. This is a day for courage and strength and conviction and faith. This is the day the Lord has made and from our tragedy we must arise to face all its implications. This is the day the Gospel of Jesus Christ must be preached with conviction and power.

A radio commentator asked men of the armed forces who for two long years had been far removed from home and country, what the men were thinking about and talking about as they spent weary days and nights preparing for an enemy which never appeared. Without a moment's hesitation, a young lad spoke up and said: "We were thinking and talking about religion, about politics, and the future." Yes, that was the answer: about their responsibilities to God and His church first; about their country and their duties towards it; and about their own lives in the tomorrow which they hoped might be theirs and their place in the life they must face together.

Every day now I am receiving letters from chaplains and officers and men stationed in the far corners of the earth. Not one of them fails to tell me of the day of reckoning we shall have to face, if, when our sons return, we shall have failed while they are away to help build a new world in which they may in peace seek gainful employment, where they may live in security with their loved ones from whom they have been separated for so long, and if we do not provide for them a church home alive to the implications of their desperate needs, and dedicated to the supreme task day and night of keeping them and theirs close to God.

They have faced God. They know the fear of death. They want pastors who, like their chaplains, are willing to share burdens and agonies of soul with them. They want a church which recognizes the desperate need of men everywhere and which is willing and passionately eager to share with others blessings which are ours, and bring to them a Savior who has known before them and knows now the depth of the suffering of the Calvary which has been theirs.

There are the social needs to be met and social evils to be eradicated. There is a delinquency problem crying out to heaven for solution. There are problems of world reconstruction and of individual rehabilitation. There is a starving world to be fed.

There are new frontiers to be crossed everywhere,

home and foreign mission tasks which stagger the imagination. There are communities and lands where our people and others have never been before which now are crying out for the gospel of Jesus Christ.

There are educational difficulties such as our fathers could never foresee with men and women to face who have become suddenly mature far beyond their years.

There are new economies looming ahead which will dwarf into insignificance the circumscribed economies of yesteryear, and the church of Jesus Christ will have to move in and among them all, lest men's souls shrivel with greed and with new lust for power and authority.

There is the trumpet call to Christlikeness in interracial relationships and the challenge that in all our world relationships we have the mark upon our brow and upon our breast of an other-worldliness which brings into our lives the mind of Jesus Christ.

There is the call to faith—abiding, convincing, convicting, and victorious faith. For without faith to move worlds we cannot see God.

So there must be in our service today a memorial of our indebtedness to a past that is gone with its inspiring memory of great deeds and great men. There must be in our service today the challenge to us for even greater deeds, greater courage, enlarged vision, and strong faith. But, if we are to measure up to the intentions of this hour, there must be, too, the trumpet call sounded from God to decision and to dedication. For if God help us not in this hour to decide for Him, and if there be not in our resolve the dedication to give ourselves with all we are and all we hope to be into His hands who controls the destinies of men and peoples and directs the history even of eternity into channels which will serve His divine purposes, then there will be in this service and in our resolve only the hollowness of empty words and the futility of despair. Only God can cope victoriously with the problems which beset us and the world, and they can be solved only as we yield ourselves willingly into His guiding hand who knows both the way and the end to which it leads.

The men who have builded the church and the world have been men who believed in God, who trusted the promise of His Word, and who walked in the footsteps of their Master, the Lord Jesus Christ. The men who will lead us from the chaos of our tragic mistakes back to the straight paths of the Kingdom of God will be the men who believe implicitly in the miraculous power of God, and the forgiving grace and mercy of God, and in the saving love of Him who walked the ways of death that we might live.

But it is the priests of God who must lead the way.

It was priests of God who did the unbelievable in the days when God led against the walled city of Jericho, that ancient citadel of sin. It was priests of God who did the bidding of God, though it seemed so impossible as to belong in the category of the absurd. It was priests of God who led the people around the walled city seven times, and seven times again the seventh day. It was priests of God who lifted the trumpets of God and sounded the trumpets so the miracle of God could be accomplished, and the city and all its evil people be utterly destroyed.

It is priests of God who have always been asked by God to do the impossible.

It was the priests of God who came to the people of God to tell them of their sins against God and of God's judgment against sin.

It was a priest of God who came out from the Jordan bottoms to cry out to the people of God: "Repent ye for the Kingdom of heaven is at hand." It was this same priest of God who stood at the threshold of the New Testament day and, pointing to Christ, cried with the trumpet voice of eternity: "Behold the Lamb of God which taketh away the sin of the world."

It was a great priest of God, who had previously blasphemed and killed, who in the power of God went through the ancient kingdoms of the world, laid the foundations of the Kingdom of God, sounded everywhere the trumpet of God, and then went the way of a martyr's death back home to God as the prophets of God have a way of doing.

It was a priest of God sounding again the trumpet of the Gospel of Jesus Christ who changed a whole world four centuries ago, and who laid the foundations of a new Kingdom of God in which you and I today have membership.

It was a priest of God who a few years ago was the first to sound the warning trumpet note against a new barbarism against which we are fighting now. They put Martin Niemoller in prison, but his trumpet call has been heard around the world.

It was a priest of God who stood before the closed doors of the Cathedral Church of Trondheim a Palm Sunday morning just a couple of years ago. In the presence of the armed might of despotism he lifted the trumpet to sound the call to his people to be faithful to God. And like an answer from the ransomed hosts of heaven the congregations shouted back their newborn faith: "A mighty fortress is our God!"

It was a priest of God who sounded the trumpet call to the Danish Church and people a few months ago. His enemies killed Kaj Munk and left his martyred body to rot in a wayside ditch. But more than the Danes have heard his call. Over and beyond the borders of his country the echo of his call has gone, till now all the world has heard the message, and men and women everywhere recognize that here was a great prophet of God calling to a world to return to God.

It is time that we listen, and listening, believe that we too must be priests of God and lead our people back to the foot of His cross who has redeemed us all with His precious blood, and who waits now to be Lord of all.

"Lift up ye gates and be ye lifted up ye everlasting doors, for the King of Glory is returning to reign." And lift ye His trumpets, ye priests of God, and sound ye out the glad refrain: The Lord of Hosts is with us. His Kingdom shall have no end.

It was the morning of last Easter day. In the darkness of the hour before dawn, I stumbled across the California hills, till at last I could look down upon the miracle which is called the Hollywood Bowl Easter sunrise service. Thirty thousand people crowded its open spaces. Thirty thousand people sang praises to the crucified but risen Lord.

Suddenly in the silence which was to hail the dawn of resurrection morn, every light was dimmed, and amphitheatre and hills and all were enveloped in enshrouding darkness.

How startled we were when a blinding flash of artificial light was thrown against an overhanging cliff to reveal a row of angel-like creatures clad in flowing garments of shining white. And then we saw the miracle. As if they heard the voice of God, they lifted their silver trumpets and sounded forth the trumpets of God, the call to worship the resurrected King.

And the dawn came. And the first rays of the sun of Easter and resurrection day. And the symphony orchestra and the great chorus joined in the triumphant Hallelujahs to our Lord. And all the trumpets of God sounded from the other side in praise of Him who liveth forever!

Trumpets of God! Trumpets of God! Oh, listen and hear! For even now they are all sounding from the other side—where God is—and where He shall be the God of all those that are His!

God's trumpet wakes the slumb'ring world:
Now, each man to his post!
The red-cross banner is unfurl'd:
Who joins the glorious host?
He who, in fealty to the truth,
And counting all the cost,
Doth consecrate his gen'rous youth—
He joins the noble host!

He who, no anger on his tongue,
Nor any idle boast,
Bears steadfast witness 'gainst all wrong—
He joins the sacred host!
He who, with calm, undaunted will,
Ne'er counts the battle lost,
But, though defeated, battles still—
He joins the faithful host!

He who is ready for the cross,
The cause despised loves most;
And shuns not pain or shame or loss—
He joins the martyr host!
God's trumpet wakes the slumb'ring world:
Now, each man to his post!
The red-cross banner is unfurl'd:
Who joins the glorious host?

("God's Trumpet Wakes the Slumbering World" by Samuel
Longfellow. From *Think on These Things,* copyright The
Beacon Press, Boston, Massachusetts.)

"He shall send his angels with a great sound of a trumpet, and they shall gather together his elect from the four
winds, from one end of heaven to the other" (Matthew
24:31).

Worship God

Fʀᴏᴍ the lofty towers of a great Gothic cathedral the bells sounded, calling a city together to worship God. High into the heavens above the twin spires reached, almost, it seemed, up to the throne of God. Fascinated I looked at this great temple, an architect's dream come true after centuries of never-ceasing, painstaking work on the part of master craftsmen, dedicated to a great task as only these artisans could be in an age which produced them. Like a huge, carved mountain, gloriously fashioned, with high-reaching Gothic lines, it stood there that day, a monument to man's search for God and worship of the living God.

The bells tolled and tolled. But they did not sound like bells at all. Rather like a celestial organ; and the bells were like the resonant voice of diapason pipes, deep in their melodious beauty: Kling, klang, kling, klang; Ding, dong, ding, dong; Come to God, Worship God, Come—to—God!

In worshipful awe I entered this temple that day and for hours and hours I sat enraptured in its cloistered atmosphere. Silent was my voice; but my heart sang its voiceless anthems to God. Never had I seen a cathedral

like this. I had visited other architectural masterpieces
before, many of them. St. Giles and York; Chester and
Herford; Gloucester and Canterbury; Westminster Ab-
bey and St. Paul's; St. Gudule's and Notre Dame; San
Chapello and the Madeleine Basilica; Trondheim and
Upsala; the Berliner Dom and St. Lawrence; St. Stephen
in Vienna and Zwingli's Cathedral in Zurich; St. Mark's
of Venice, and the Duomo in Florence; St. Paul's and St.
Peter, St. John's Lateran and Sancta Maria Maggiore in
Rome; the Cathedrals of Pisa and of Milan, and many,
many others. But never had my soul been stirred with
deep emotion and lifted with celestial visions as it was
that day I beheld the glories of the cathedral of Cologne
and heard its bells calling a forgetful world to worship
God.

Yes, I know, its worship had been debased and its purpose distorted. Men are forever dishonoring God, though
they think their man-made ceremonies are designed to
exalt His Name. But here a sincere soul could forget all
this, if he looked only at the design of the temple and
forgot the intentions of those who had so long substituted
a religious service which failed to give the glory due to
the Christ of God.

All the while the bells tolled and their message was as
a call from God: Kling, klang; ding, dong; Come to God!
Come—to—God!

I looked about me and into the vaulted ceilings of this
temple whose erection had been accomplished only at the
cost of centuries of time. How high they were! How far
up they reached—up—up—almost up to God. I looked and
looked and at last I thought I understood the language
of those lofty Gothic pillars and those high pointed
arches. As I looked they suddenly changed—all of them.
And all I could see at last were the upstretched arms of a
people seeking God, arms and hands lifted high, to be
clasped by folded hands as if they were lifted up in

prayer. Gothic pillars and arches—and then arms lifted and hands folded as if in prayer. How impressive it was! A temple of God; an architecture whose pull was up; a people seeking God; arms raised high; hands folded as if in prayer!

And the bells rang on and on: Come to God! Worship God! Come—to—God!

It was a glorious day. The sun was shining brightly, its blazing light full of promise and of hope. Through ecclesiastical glass windows whose manufacture must have cost a fortune, whose art has now been hopelessly lost, the slanting rays poured to converge at last, as the architects must have visioned they would, upon the high altar which in its emblazoned glory looked like the throne of God. Shafts of sunlight carrying the rainbow colors of the windows through which they had entered blazing upon the altar of God as though it were heaped with jewels from heaven. Round about and stacked in great clusters were the lighted candle tapers adding an eerie background of deflected glory!

Then suddenly, unexpectedly, majestically the great organ in the lofty gallery burst forth into a melodious chorus of rapturous glory. Softly at first, like the quiet breath of coming spring, then joyfully, rapturously, ecstatically, it sounded forth its song of triumph, like some celestial symphonic orchestra playing its praises to God. I listened and listened. Its song was like the inspired "Kamenoi Ostrow"—Easter Bells—of Anton Rubinstein —full of melodious harmony and triumphant ecstasy.

And then I saw a miracle. The sun shone. The music sounded. Shafts of jeweled sunlight played upon the altar of God. Suddenly—oh, it could not be! But yes! Suddenly I saw and beheld a procession of angels marching majestically down all these beams of jeweled light, down and down, till converging before the altar which was the throne of God they kneeled in adoring worship. In their

arms were great branches of palms. In their clasped hands
great clusters of Easter lilies. They sang as they marched,
sang and sang and sang: Praise be to God; praise be to
God; praise be to God! And the bells of the cathedral
tolled and tolled: Kling, klang; Kling, klang; Ding, dong;
Ding, dong! Come to God! Worship God! Come—to—
God!

At last an endless host of white-clad visitors from the
land of angels were standing before the throne. From the
midst of the throne a voice was speaking: "I am the
resurrection and the life: he that believeth in me, though
he were dead, yet shall he live: And whosoever liveth and
believeth in me shall never die."

Silent was this temple as the words sounded forth. But
only for a moment. Then in triumphant chorus the celestial host, crowded there before the throne, sounded the
trumpets of God and sang in chords of celestial glory:
"Worthy is the Lamb that was slain to receive power, and
riches, and wisdom, and strength, and honor, and glory,
and blessing." Lifted high were their palms; stretched
aloft their lilies. Back and forth, forth and back, they
marched singing as they went. Always singing. And bow-
ing low as they passed the throne of God. Oh, how they
sang! My heart was near to bursting with the glory of the
celestial music, as it sounded forth before the throne of
God.

At last the music reached its climax as it does in Rubinstein's masterpiece. More exultant was its cadence. More
triumphant its melody. More ecstatic its spirit of worship.
The great organ sounded through its many pipes. Celestial orchestras took up the strain. The temple bells and
all the bells of heaven were proclaiming the Easter message of resurrection and life and power. The angels sang
and sang. The bells rang and rang. The trumpets of God
joined in the triumphant finale. Till all at once, standing
there before God's throne, the angels prostrated them-

selves again before the Lamb of God in worship and adoration. But their palms were lifted high—and the Easter lilies.

As I looked and looked in awe, I beheld the final miracle of it all. Prostrated before the throne, the angels had fallen in the form of a great cross. And as I looked, I could see their faces or their forms or their wings no more. They seemed to have vanished as suddenly as they had come. But the lilies were there and the palms, and their form as they lay there together was the form of a cross before the altar of God. A cross on which died the Savior of the world. But the cross was a great bed of lilies, Easter lilies, and their open faces smiled and laughed with hope and joy and happiness and peace as if in the presence of God.

Above me and about me there was a strange silence now and a strange peace. God was with men. And His hands touched the soul burdened with sin and set it free.

Then the bells began tolling and tolling again, calling a world to come to God for rest: Kling, klang; Kling, klang; Ding, dong! Ding, dong! I heard them say. But there was joy in their voices now, joy and peace.

> Kling klang! Kling, klang!
> Ding, dong! Ding, dong!
> Come to God!
> Worship God!
> Come—to God!—God!—God!
> ....to God!

And all the trumpets of God sounded forth in triumph and in victory and in celestial praise from the other side. And angels and archangels sang the new song before the throne of God:

> "Worship God!
> Worship God!" (Rev. 22:9).